As I Journey On

Meditations for Those Facing Death

Sharon Dardis

and

Cindy Rogers

Augsburg

MINNEAPOLIS

AS I JOURNEY ON
Meditations for Those Facing Death

Cover design by Nicole Sletten
Cover image © Tony Stone Images. Used by permission.
Book design by Michelle L. Norstad

Library of Congress Cataloging-in-Publication Data
Dardis, Sharon, 1949–
  As I journey on: meditations for those facing death / Sharon Dardis and Cindy Rogers.
    p. cm.
  Includes bibliographical references and index.
  ISBN 0-8066-3889-3 (alk. paper)
    1. Terminally ill—Religious life. 2. Death—Religious Life—Meditations. I. Rogers, Cindy, 1950– II. Title.

BL625.9.S53 D37 2000
155.9'37—dc21   99-52772

Manufactured in the U.S.A.   AF 9-3889

04   03   02   01   00   1   2   3   4   5   6   7   8   9   10

CONTENTS

For Cindy's mother, Shirley,
whose quest for a book to help her
in her journey was the impetus for this project.
For friends, family, and acquaintances
who shared their stories and understood
that the healing is in the telling.
For the dying and their loved ones,
whose journeys teach us all.

PREFACE

This book is intended to be a collection of meditations for those facing death. Its impetus came from a dying mother's request for "a book that meets me where I'm at." Shirley understood the process of life and death as a journey from one stage to the next. As she struggled with the biological and psychological functions of dying, she also hungered for conversation and nourishment of her mind. She wanted dialogue, lessons, and stories about those who had gone before her. In a world that usually avoids the topic, she wanted to talk about her own dying.

As I Journey On: Meditations for Those Facing Death was written to offer such tools for facing the reality of your own or someone else's death. If you, like Shirley, are seeking true stories and thoughtful insights about death and dying, these thoughts may help you in your own journey. The meditations are meant to be read one at a time, in order for you to fully process their contents. They may challenge your mind even as they bring you comfort and may help you to live more intentionally through your own living and dying days.

If you know your life is limited or if it stretches unknowingly before you, carry this collection of meditations with you on your journey. Be a prepared traveler and rest often in the words, the stories, and their lessons. Like Shirley, you too can be a seeker of hopeful insights. Our wish is that these stories may nourish you on your travels, ease the way to your final destination, and meet you wherever you happen to be along the way.

REMEMBER ME

WHAT SHE COULD OFFER GEORGE WAS FAR MORE
THAN WHAT HAD HAPPENED—A CERTAIN SEQUENCE
THAT WOULD LEAD HIM TO THE CORE OF THE STORY, A
STORY THAT WOULD HOLD AN ENTIRE WORLD.

—URSULA HEGI

My mother, Shirley, was not a storyteller. She was grounded in the reality of her days—sixty-nine years of them—teaching, farming, parenting. When it was Shirley's turn to die, she didn't want small talk or get-well wishes, she wanted remembrances. She often asked her family and her friends to refresh her memory and remind her of past times together. She wanted to recall the good times and the bad, and all the times between. More than that, she needed to think about them, ponder them, sort through them; she wanted them offered up for her analysis so she could decide where she stood in their midst. Perhaps even more than that, she wanted those who offered the stories to think about her, to remember her with some detail and clarity of thought. She didn't want her visitors to remember her illness . . . no, not at all. She wanted them to remember the work, the play, the crises, the trips, the special and important times. She wanted to remember and be remembered for the stories they'd shared.

The smallest stories sometimes meant the most. "Shirley, I'll never forget your wedding, that ninety-degree August day, when nearly everyone in the church stuck to the newly varnished pews." "Mom, do you remember the time I ran away from home and you told me I could go, but I'd have to leave my clothes behind, because you'd invested a lot of time in sewing each and every one? I was so shocked that you'd let me go without clothes that I couldn't run away after all." "Grandma, do you remember the time we went biking around the city? I was only six. You kept turning around to see if I was following you and riding safely next to the curb. Suddenly you plowed right into a parked car! After that, I guess we knew who was the safer biker." Stories gave value and richness to Shirley's final days.

There's an old story about a rabbi who went to a certain spot in a forest, built a fire in a specific way, and uttered a special prayer, asking for a miracle to save his people from a disaster. His people were saved. Generations later, a second rabbi went to the forest to ask for a miracle to save his people. He couldn't recall how to build the fire or all the words to the prayer, but he hoped what he knew would be enough. And so it was. Generations later, a third rabbi, burdened with the problems of his people, sat in a chair in his living room. He didn't know the place, the fire, or the prayer, but he knew the story, and that was sufficient.

Stories are often all we have of any real substance. Sometimes, stories are all we have to live by . . . and to die by. Stories have power. They can save and redeem lives. They can offer a model, a message, a warm embrace, a cup of humor, a bottle of compassion, a pot of inspiration or hope, a moment of truth. The sharing of stories allows us memorable glimpses into the lives of others and into the legacies of our own lives.

Ursula Hegi, in her novel *Stones From the River*, says that a story can lead to a core. A story can "hold an entire world. It has to do with what to tell first—though it hadn't happened first—and what to end the story with. It has to do with what to enhance and what to relinquish. And what to embrace."

Shirley didn't care in which order the stories came to her over the course of her last six weeks. But she was hungry for them. She sought not only her own stories, but those of others. Stories that would help her grapple with the life she was now living, confined to a few rooms. The books she'd always enjoyed didn't meet her needs anymore. She wanted different stories. She embraced and pondered the bits and pieces given to her. We wish there'd been even more for her. This collection is part of the legacy of her journey, and a part of the legacies of many others, a core that we hope will only grow as you, the reader, ponder your own stories.

Prayer

O Great Spirit, the holder of all the stories in the universe, remind me of the power of stories—the stories I've read and heard and lived. Open my eyes and mind so that I may take in the power or feel the inspiration or discern the truth that is waiting for me in stories. Stretch my memory so that I can grasp my own stories and remember that they hold power for others. Amen.

Question to Ponder

Which of my personal stories is particularly meaningful or memorable to me? Why?

Today I Will

Pass along a story.

LESSONS

TEACH ME TO DIE. HOLD ON TO MY HAND.

I HAVE SO MANY QUESTIONS; THINGS I DON'T
UNDERSTAND.

TEACH ME TO DIE. GIVE ALL YOU CAN GIVE.

IF YOU'LL TEACH ME OF DYING, I WILL TEACH YOU
TO LIVE!

—DEANNA EDWARDS

My father used to dip his hands in melted wax. It was a therapeutic measure intended to relieve the pain in his arthritic swollen joints. As a seven-year-old, I understood it more as an exercise in art. Once the wax cooled and hardened, Dad let me peel off the layers. Or better yet, he would gently work his hands free and hand me a paraffin glove, intact and ready to insert over my own much smaller and healthier fingers. This memory is a comforting one for me. I remember the smells and the warmth of the kitchen we sat in, the tolerant smile of my mother as Dad and I created yet another mess, and even the laughter of my father as I danced around the table with a pale glove that, only moments before, had held his chronic pain.

I don't remember anyone mentioning he was dying, but in reality he was—from rheumatic heart disease and its debilitating symptoms. In fact, the whole while I was growing up, he was slowly letting go. Even when he finally died when I was fourteen, it took a long time for me to recognize that in his dying and how he coped were lessons that had shaped me as a person. The lessons are revealed even today, thirty-four years later, as I continue to process his death and the meaning of the gifts he left me.

Without formal education or therapy or studying any books written on the subject of "dignity" or "grace" under adversity, my father demonstrated how it was done. He laughed a lot. He was skinny but swollen, blotchy, and frail. He would make silly faces and I would laugh. He took out his ill-fitting dentures and embarrassed me in front of my friends. They loved him and said he was funny.

My father enjoyed music and would strum his battered guitar as he sang melodies I grew to love. One old country song was a favorite of mine. "This Old House" was recorded in 1954 and made popular by Rosemary Clooney. For years after Dad died, I sang it from memory. One day, while singing to my children, I paid closer attention to the lyrics and realized the words spoke of where Dad knew he was headed.

Ain't a-gonna need this house no longer
Ain't a-gonna need this house no more
Ain't got time to fix the shingles
Ain't got time to fix the floor
Ain't got time to oil the hinges
Nor to mend the windowpane
Ain't a-gonna need this house no longer
I'm a gettin' ready to meet the saints

Dad never spoke to me of dying; he just sang. My father hoped and persevered and, in his physical weakness, grew stronger spiritually. He grew beautiful flowers and a prolific vegetable garden, and nurtured rabbits, pigeons, and miniature roosters in our barn out back.

I wasn't with him at the hospital when he died. My mother said his last words were "I want to go home." He might've been talking about meeting those saints he'd sung about in Rosemary Clooney's song, but I decided later that he'd meant his earthly home as well because it was where he'd taught us, loved us, and created memories. Although home was the place he'd lived with his disease, it was also a haven of unexpected gifts both for him and for his family.

The pain of his arthritis had given the beauty of waxen gloves. The physical weakness of a debilitating illness had offered the chance of living each day vigorously. Dad loved his home, and I'm not surprised that, at the moment of death, he wanted to be there. That's where I was when I heard he'd died, in our backyard, with his flowers and vegetables, the barn full of animals, and his lessons. I learned from my dying father that we are all dying; some faster than others, and some with more or less grace. What matters is to recognize that in the process of living until we die, we teach each other, and that those lessons, in retrospect, should comfort us. In my memories, I sometimes slip once again into my father's waxen gloves, remember his lessons, and thank him. And that's comfort enough, I suppose. I believe we taught one another.

PRAYER

O God, help me be aware of the lessons I am teaching, as I am both living and dying. Grant me the wisdom that comes from suffering and love. Give me the opportunity to teach others the lessons of letting go with a gentle spirit. Grant me peace in my questioning and a hand to hold in my journey. Amen.

QUESTION TO PONDER

What lesson am I learning in my journey?

TODAY I WILL

Hold a loved one's hand and share one life lesson I believe we've taught one another.

SCARS

THE FRIENDS WHO MEAN THE MOST TO US ARE THOSE
WHO, INSTEAD OF GIVING ADVICE, SOLUTIONS, OR
CURES, HAVE CHOSEN RATHER TO SHARE OUR PAIN
AND TOUCH OUR WOUNDS WITH A WARM AND TEN-
DER HAND.

—HENRI NOUWEN

"May I see your scar?" asked Linda's best friend, bustling around Linda's living room, as if she were very much at home with medical procedures. Although it had been several weeks since the surgery, Linda certainly didn't feel at home with herself. This surgery was the only time she'd been in the hospital since the birth of her last child, nineteen years earlier. Ruth's request took her by surprise. In fact, it took her breath away. She was a private person. She hadn't enjoyed all the hands-on administering of the hospital personnel or the sudden appearance of company at her hospital-room door. And now this—a friend wanting to see the incision across her abdomen. She avoided looking at it herself. It was too new. The whole idea of cancer was new. Linda gazed at Ruth, a woman she'd known and trusted for many years. Okay. Maybe together they could look at it. Maybe then the scar and all it represented could be discussed matter-of-factly. Maybe its ramifications—laid right out there in the open—could be, in some way, diminished.

Whether our battle scars are on the inside, next to our heart, or on the outside, across our abdomen, they are diffi-cult to reveal—especially if the outcome is still in question. We'd rather hide them away, pretending that life is not only okay, but pretty darn good. We don't want to appear to be in a weakened state. The images of vitality, strength, and future are incredibly important to us.

Why is that? Why do we expend so much energy hiding our wounds, pretending all is "normal," when in fact our world has been turned upside down? For decades now, the medical world has looked at serious illness, dying, and even aging as medical failures, rather than nature's way. The media perpetuates the idea of youthful vitality in their ad campaigns. We seem to live in a society where wellness is considered success and illness is failure.

One woman wrote in her journal: "Once, rising from a chair was a graceful thing. Now getting to my feet is a bitter thing, and I know no one wants to watch me struggle, let alone be seen with a woman who must use a walker." A young man confessed his fear to his doctor: "I can't accept being weak. I'm so angry. And I don't know what to do. I cry over every little thing. I can't control my emotions. The thought of what is going on inside my body is terrifying."

In a hospital or a hospice setting, we don't have to pretend to be strong. In these places, people know we're sick and in a serious condition. And in truth, it takes far more energy *not* to talk about what's going on inside us than the other way around. But even there, it's a struggle. Like the father who talked to his dying daughter about her flowers, the weather, her friends, her radio . . . and then he'd go out in the hallway and cry. Finally, after the intervention of a compassionate doctor, they talked about her scars, her dying. Their last days together were enriched.

Although baring one's scars—and admitting to the emotions that go along with them—is a nerve-racking ordeal, once they're exposed, one is able to deal with them more effectively. The best way to make sense out of a major shift in our lives is to plunge in and move with it. And suddenly—maybe *because* of our courage to say something— someone else shows a scar, too. And then we realize the truth: these scars are not signs of weakness, but badges of courage.

And Linda? Well, she showed her abdominal scar to her friend. Ruth touched it with a tender hand. They examined its details, talked about the surgery and about cancer. They talked about her fears and worries. Linda was glad she'd made the extra effort the showing required. "I felt so much better afterward. Lighter. More resolved. Even hopeful. Carrying around that scar hasn't been as scary since."

PRAYER

I feel like damaged goods. Lord, if I can't be healed through divine intervention, then send me someone who isn't afraid to hold my hand and touch my wounds. Send someone who's willing to accept me as powerless, fearful, weak, and in pain, but who still sees the real me beneath the scars. I am more than my weakened body. Amen.

QUESTION TO PONDER

Do I have scars I've hidden away? Can I show one?

TODAY I WILL

Be grateful for anyone who sits beside me, ready to listen if I choose to share.

ℒℐ𝒱ℐℕ𝒢 𝓕𝒰ℒℒ𝒴

LIFE IS NO BRIEF CANDLE TO ME. IT IS A SORT OF SPLEN-
DID TORCH WHICH I'VE GOT TO HOLD UP FOR THE
MOMENT, AND I WANT TO MAKE IT BURN AS BRIGHTLY
AS POSSIBLE BEFORE HANDING IT ON TO FUTURE GEN-
ERATIONS.

—GEORGE BERNARD SHAW

Tom was a middle-aged, western-North Dakota cowboy, ruggedly handsome, with hair graying at the temples and a few facial scars that lent him character. He wore his gray Stetson tilted just slightly over his sun-tanned face. His eyes twinkled from beneath its brim as he reminded you that he was one hundred percent Irish and had the luck to prove it. He wore cowboy boots because they kept his feet firmly anchored in the stirrups of his favorite saddle. He drove a battered pickup truck to feed his cows, take his wife to dinner, or attend weekly mass. He was a man's man: full of life, and strong from years of manual labor. He was quick to tell you that he'd never been seriously ill, and he took pride in hard work and his diverse work experiences: as a teacher in a one-room school, a rancher, farmer, brand inspector, and county sheriff.

Tom had recently retired from his thirty-year career in law enforcement when he was diagnosed with kidney cancer. He died a year later, at the age of sixty. Yet his last year of life remained the most vivid in the minds of his friends and family. Not for the disease process itself or for Tom's courage in the face of suffering, although those may have been part of it. He is remembered for his fighting spirit and for the way he lived his last days with a passionate determination to not give in to his disease. Some may have called it

15

denial. And although, in his quiet cowboy way, he never spoke of it directly, this stubborn philosophy followed him everywhere that last year of his life. Sometimes it frustrated his wife and confused his friends. He refused, however, to admit he was dying. Instead, he renewed old goals and prepared for yet another good fight, intending to fully live each day until he died.

The day after Tom received his diagnosis and understood the treatment odds he was facing, he decided to come out of retirement and run again for a third term as county sheriff. His family thought it was a foolish decision. "Why not conserve your strength?" they asked. "What will you tell the voters? Think of the energy it will take!" His stern look said that this was nonnegotiable, so they ordered campaign flyers with last year's picture on them and reminded voters of his excellent record in law enforcement. His family picked up Tom's "brightly burning torch" and tried to carry it as their own, although the reality of the disease made it difficult for them to stay hopeful. Tom requested the details of his illness be concealed from everyone but his closest family. He was convinced that this, too, was a battle he could win. Family and friends respected Tom's fighting spirit, but their looks to one another said they wondered how much longer he could sustain this pace in the face of his disease. The harder Tom worked, however, the more alive he felt and, again, his "splendid torch" burned brightly.

The following November, Tom won the election for sheriff. It was a bittersweet victory, because by election day it was apparent he would never be well enough to serve. He was dying, and everyone in the county was well aware of that. Yet the community had voted for him. It was a show of support that said they understood he wasn't ready to quit yet, and they honored and respected that decision.

Tom might have died then. But he had more to live for: to spend Thanksgiving, Christmas, and one last wedding anniversary with his wife and family. So he sat in his recliner by the sunny dining-room window, quietly accepting visitors who had come to pay their respects. Often there was no conversation. Tom summoned the strength to smile or nod; his guests sat hunched in a chair beside him, twirling their hats or nervously twisting their pocketbook handles. It was difficult for Tom to say good-bye; it was hard work. Still, he was fighting the good fight and winning, simply because he chose to be there.

On December 28, the day after Tom's thirtieth wedding anniversary, his grown children, his beloved grandchildren, and his wife remained close by. Tom was actively dying. He seemed aware of that and still would not verbalize it. His acceptance of death was held at bay with his desire to live even these last hours as he chose. He was still in charge. So he spoke, with much difficulty, to his grown sons and their families. "You should go home now," he said. And they did.

Tom died at home early the next morning with his wife at his side. His third term of office as county sheriff would have begun that same week. Although he never fulfilled that final role, he is remembered as the sheriff who won the election and lost his life, but never ever lost his ability to fully live.

PRAYER

O God, help me to work hard at living life to its fullest measure. Give me strength to burn my torch brightly, even at life's end. Amen.

QUESTION TO PONDER

What can I do to live fully today?

TODAY I WILL

Rejoice in a task that will help me illuminate my life to its fullest measure.

CHARACTER

THE CHARACTER OF OUR LIFE IS THE CHARACTER OF

OUR DYING; BOTH ARE PART OF ONE PROCESS.

—STANLEY KELEMAN

Janet's primary job during her lifetime was that of a stay-at-home mom, but she liked to acknowledge the period when she was a secretary for 20th Century Fox in Minneapolis. It was a time of wide black hats and veils, and Janet wore them with flair. Not college educated, but a woman of quick wit, Janet wouldn't allow her daughter to flaunt her degree without a rejoinder. "So that's what a right angle is," she would say, and mimic her daughter's visual example by pointing to the bent elbow of her left arm. "Well then, this must be a left angle."

At the age of fifty-eight, Janet was diagnosed with terminal cancer. In spite of the poor prognosis, she went through radiation and chemotherapy, determined to make it to her niece's wedding on June 21. Betsy's wedding became her ultimate goal, for it promised a grand reunion of Janet's side of the family. In the first week of June, accompanied by her mother, daughter, and a wheelchair, Janet went shopping for a dress. Surprising her daughter, she bought the most expensive dress and shoes she'd ever owned. "Well, you can always bury me in it," she said in a spirited, determined voice.

By June 21, Janet's kidneys were shutting down and her legs were swollen—too swollen to wear her beautiful shoes. But she pulled the new dress over her eighty-two-pound body, donned a fetching red hat, and went to the wedding. She was excited to be there. With pride she watched her six-year-old grandson carry the rings down the aisle. At the reception, she glimpsed relatives in every corner of the hall.

But as the evening wore on, Janet became quieter, more pensive. "No one is coming over to talk to me. Don't they know I can't easily go to them?" She eyed her cousins, her aunts and sisters, her nephews and nieces expectantly. "I think they're afraid. They don't know what to say." With great effort, she arose and walked unsteadily to her kin. Despite the awkward, nervous, tongue-tied greeting of her cousin George, she asked him, "And why aren't we out there dancing?" And they danced. To smooth the way to talking about deeper health issues, Janet asker her sister, "And how are your knees these days, Emma?"

Janet could easily have become angry or slipped into self-pity. She would have had every right. Of all the people who'd come that day, she'd made the most valiant effort. For Janet, the wedding was not just another event; it was the final event. But with wisdom she understood the situation, and with courage she showed her family how to do it, how to live one's dying days with dignity, grace, even a sense of fun and flair—gifts that required a great deal of her waning strength. Five days later, Janet died.

Few of us know how to die, let alone model it. None of us know what our own dying days will be like. But we do know that there's not just one right way to die; there are many right ways to die. Just as one person's life is like no other person's life, so one person's death is like no other's. Joan Conner, in *Loss of the Ground Note*, wrote "There is no right response to death. You make it up as you go along." Janet, dressed with style, applauded her grandson, and taught her relatives how to talk to her by coming at them sideways. She danced and asked them questions, and soon they were talking, laughing, and once again enjoying her company. By the end of the evening, they were able to say good-bye in a meaningful way.

John Tully Carmody's goal was to finish writing a book during his dying days, a good majority of which he spent in the hospital. One of his commentaries included a glimpse of another patient's courage in the middle of a hospital corridor. "I watched a woman come out of her treatment, then square her shoulders and grin at her daughter. . . . She was still more than her woe." And so it is with each of us: we wish to be more than our troubles, our misfortunes, our illnesses. From time to time, we need to rise above our situations and surprise those around us with our wit and charm, our grace and wisdom, our energy and courage. It will give them something extra to hold on to after we're gone.

PRAYER

O God, I'd like to be more than my woe, but I don't know if I have the stamina. Some days I can barely function. Please give me the push to rise above my disease, my weakened body, my pain, so that I might model—in some small way—how to live until I die. Amen.

QUESTION TO PONDER

What can I share about dying that will help those around me understand this journey and feel more ease about talking to me?

TODAY I WILL

Set one tiny, mediocre, or grand goal.

FINAL WISHES

IF EVEN DYING IS TO BE MADE A SOCIAL FUNCTION,
THEN, PLEASE, GRANT ME THE FAVOR OF SNEAKING
OUT ON TIPTOE WITHOUT DISTURBING THE PARTY.

—DAG HAMMARSKJÖLD

Some might agree with Dag Hammarskjöld and argue that these days, we are trying to make dying too much of a "social event." Perhaps there are those who want a more private death, not wishing to discuss their thoughts and feelings about end-of-life issues. More and more, however, advocates for the terminally ill are encouraging open communication between caregivers and the person who is ill. Yet it isn't easy to talk about things like death and dying, especially when it's our own or a loved one's death we may be discussing. Sometimes people refuse or are unable to ever fully accept or acknowledge the fact that they are dying; they aren't able to have those conversations at all. How important is it to share final wishes and talk about personal concerns when you are facing your own impending death? Can it be helpful even if it is painful and difficult to do? Can one express last wishes and still leave this life without "disturbing the party"?

Canadian experts recently conducted a study of patients with life-threatening illnesses. The research team was looking for ways to improve the quality of care at end-of-life. They asked a variety of patients questions about what was most important to them when thinking about their own death. Number one on the list was to avoid needless prolonging of life. Many feared being kept alive on machines without quality of life when there was no hope of recovery.

Second was the need to have some control about the care and the decisions regarding their treatments. They didn't need total control of every situation but rather wanted their requests regarding end-of-life to be known, respected, and followed. Third, they feared being a burden to their loved ones and thought the way to avoid that might be to make their wishes known while they were still able to discuss them. That way the difficult decisions could be made while they were still able to offer input. Fourth, they wanted their families to talk to them about dying. Even as they acknowledged it was a hard subject to talk about, they felt it was important to be open and honest. Last, the patients wanted to be assured of adequate pain and symptom control. Every one of these "final wishes" can be made known with good communication. It is possible to be in control of your final days of life by discussing your specific concerns with family and medical staff who will listen while there is still time to do so.

Arnold R. Beisser was stricken with polio when he was twenty-five years old. It was 1950 and he was a new medical intern, preparing for a surgical residency. Prior to contracting polio, he was called to active duty for the naval reserves and had to put his medical residency on hold. While awaiting his orders, he played tennis and won a national tennis tournament. He seemed young and invincible. The polio struck suddenly, paralyzing him from the neck down and confining him to an iron lung. Forty years later, in a wheelchair and only minimally recovered, he was living a full life as a psychiatrist. He wrote a book about his disabilities called *Flying Without Wings*. In his sequel *A Graceful Passage: Notes on the Freedom to Live or Die,* Dr. Beisser wrote about death but said his intentions were that it be about a "celebration of life and all its wonders" and "it just happens that one of those wonders is death."

In April of 1990, Dr. Beisser, then sixty-four, shared his final wishes in a *Los Angeles Times* article about his latest book. He, too, was afraid of becoming a burden to others. He had signed a living will, stipulating he wanted no lifesaving measures and asked he be allowed, if possible, to die at home. He admitted he wasn't afraid of death itself but of the "process of arriving there." He wished, as we all would, to die with a minimum of pain and without using up the resources of his family. He dealt with his fears by discussing them with his wife. He said, "We need to open some healing dialogues about death." The *Los Angeles Times* article ended with Dr. Beisser talking about parties, too, just as Dag Hammarskjöld had in his book in 1964. Dr. Beisser writes: "I would like my passage to be a celebration, surrounded by those I love. We will sit together, with perhaps a toast or two. I hope we will reminisce, laugh a lot, and cry. If the party goes well, we will not be able to tell the laughter from the tears. When the last guest is gone, I will close my eyes, and quietly slip away."

PRAYER

God, I too have wishes about my own dying. Grant my loved ones and me the courage to have "healing dialogues about death." Help me to remember that dying is yet another part of living. Allow me time now to make decisions with my loved ones in conversations that will ensure my dignity and peace. Amen.

QUESTION TO PONDER

What are my "last wishes"?

TODAY I WILL

Share those wishes with someone close to me. I will begin by saying, "I am ready to talk about my final wishes today. Will you sit with me and listen?"

FEAR

OUR LORD, OUR GOD, DELIVER US FROM THE FEAR OF
WHAT MIGHT HAPPEN AND GIVE US THE GRACE TO
ENJOY WHAT NOW IS AND TO KEEP STRIVING AFTER
WHAT OUGHT TO BE.

—PETER MARSHALL

The late Walter Payton was once a 202-pound halfback for the Chicago Bears who made football history with his athletic abilities and sweet disposition. He was described as invincible. He was every football fan's hero. Yet thirteen years after he retired, when he went public with the news that he had an incurable liver disease, he said, "Hell, yeah, I'm scared. But what can I do? It's not in my hands anymore. It's in God's hands and in the doctor's hands." And then Walter Payton cried.

What fears confront us when we face the fact of our own eventual death? Charlotte Epstein, in her book *Nursing the Dying Patient,* lists a staggering fifteen items found in her research of "a checklist of fears of death and dying." Some of them include the fear that this life is all there is; death will bring the end of everything. Others are afraid of leaving the people who depend on them and making loved ones unhappy. There is the fear of not having enough time to seek forgiveness. Some worry about losing control of their body or that there will be pain with the actual moment of death. The fear of dependency is also an issue, as is the very common fear of dying alone.

Frank was a tall, thin, grandfatherly, hospice patient who was soft-spoken and rarely raised his voice. He had developed a special rapport with the hospice nurses who cared for him, quietly joking as they visited him to check his blood pressure or review his medication needs. Any discussion the nurses tried to have with Frank about his concerns or fears of dying he often brushed aside with a joke or story, as if he wanted to take the focus away from himself and the topic of death.

One day, Frank's nurse found him agitated and confused, thrashing about in bed and shouting for help. She tried calming him with her familiar voice, asking what she could bring him or if he was having pain. He did not respond and continued to struggle. Another nurse came to say he'd been medicated for pain and perhaps he was "just confused." The hospice nurse pulled a chair up close to the head of his bed and quietly began to recite the 23rd Psalm. "The Lord is my shepherd, I shall not want." Frank's arms and legs moved the bed linens up and down. "He makes me lie down in green pastures; he leads me beside still waters." Frank's eyes were pinned tightly shut; his lips stretched in a pale, thin line. "Even though I walk through the darkest valley . . ." Frank suddenly stopped thrashing. He lay very still, opened his eyes and looked directly at his nurse. Lifting his head slightly, he exclaimed, "I fear no evil!" Then he lay back quietly on the pillow and rested, his breathing became calmer, his pulse returned to normal, and his nurse sat by the bed in amazement.

Was it fear that Frank was expressing with his restlessness? That hospice nurse would argue that it was. He died quietly several hours later, with his family at his bedside. They had heard of Frank's response to the 23rd Psalm and continued to comfort him with soft recitations of familiar scripture in their own soothing voices.

Although Walter Payton was afraid, he was quoted soon before his death that he was determined to keep a positive and proactive outlook. "I'm as healthy as I can be right now. I'm going to do everything I can do. I can't lay around and mope . . . and hope everything is going to be okay. I'm still moving and grooving."

How can you, like Walter Payton did, move and groove

in the face of impending death? What can deliver you from the fear of what might happen in the future? Can you be like Frank and focus on the present, listening to words that might bring relief from worry? Is there a way to live in the present, to voice your fears, but not let them consume you? Can you cry like Walter Payton did, and then keep striving with courage and faith that everything is, after all, in God's hands?

PRAYER

Comforter of the fearful, give me courage to face each day. Allow me the honesty to name each fear I harbor. Grant those around me the ability to soothe those fears and bring me peace. Amen.

QUESTION TO PONDER

How might I move beyond my fear? Will my concerns feel less overwhelming if I talk about them with a loved one?

TODAY I WILL

Tell one person one deep-seated fear I carry within me and ask for help in conquering it.

CONTROL

HOW A PERSON DIES REVEALS MUCH ABOUT HOW HE
OR SHE LIVED.

—MILTON LOMASK

Several years ago, in a televised interview with Ted Koppel of ABC's *Nightline*, a man named Morrie Schwartz talked about dying with Lou Gehrig's disease, a relentless illness of the neurological system that gradually diminishes the victim's ability to move, eat, and, finally, breathe. But Morrie was a college professor, beloved by his students, and he wasn't about to let the most important course work of his life go by without some thought and analysis. Koppel had read about him in the *Boston Globe* and asked to interview him, thinking that the greater public might benefit from someone's frank talk about death and dying.

The two men spoke about many things, including Morrie's increasing dependency on other people for eating, sitting, and moving from place to place. Then Koppel asked, "What do you dread the most?" Morrie paused, then asked if he could say a certain thing on television. Koppel told him to go ahead. Morrie looked him in the eyes and said, "Well, one day soon someone's gonna have to wipe my ass."

Loss of control over our own bodies is a seemingly unspeakable fear, whether we're talking about serious accidents, a chronic disease, or dying. Helplessness and dependency on others for the most basic needs diminishes our self-esteem and self-worth, and it increases our guilt. Raised to be independent from the moment we take our first step, our loss of independence is devastating, especially so when there's no reprieve, and dependence begins to consume our days.

Relatives and friends don't like to face this terrible sentence on the body either. In fact, they often discount it or, worse, ignore it, as if this diminishing of the body weren't really happening to us. The feelings of loneliness and abandonment are prevalent.

We must find ways to maintain or regain some control—over our illness, its treatment, and the treatment setting. That might mean asking to go home instead of remaining in the hospital. It might mean opting for more treatment or for less. It could mean asking for control of pain medication, and the frequency of the doses. Taking back some control might mean posting a sign that says *No Visitors Please,* or it might mean filling the living room with former students, like Morrie Schwartz was prone to do. Maybe it means a frank talk with doctors or relatives about the extent of extra measures to be taken. If depression and anxiety are causing more pain than the physical problems, then a request for psychological or spiritual help is in order. Conversations with professionals may be the one way to regain our decision-making powers.

And what happened to Morrie when he finally succumbed to the thing he dreaded most? In *Tuesdays with Morrie* by Mitch Albom, Morrie tells us: "I'm an independent person, so my inclination was to fight all of this—being helped from the car, having someone else dress me. I felt a little ashamed, because our culture tells us we should be ashamed if we can't wipe our own behind. But then I figured, *forget what the culture says. I am not going to be ashamed. What's the big deal?* And you know what? The strangest thing. I began to *enjoy* my dependency. Now I enjoy when they turn me over on my side and rub cream on my behind so I don't get sores. Or when they wipe my brow or they massage my legs. I revel in it. I close my eyes and soak it up." Morrie goes on to say that it's like being a child again, that it's inside all of us. The trick was remembering how to enjoy it. He suggested that we all yearn in some way to return to those days of unconditional love, unconditional attention. The fact is that most of us didn't get enough the first time around. So, in the end, Morrie maintained the upper hand over his desperate situation—not by hating it or merely enduring it, but by reveling in the personal attention.

PRAYER

O God, can I admit aloud that this loss of control scares me and that I want it back? Assure me that it's not asking too much to want more independence, more pain relief, more control over my remaining days. Remind me that these are basic needs, and that I ask for them in order to live each day more fully. Amen.

QUESTION TO PONDER

What can I do to keep my self-worth intact?

TODAY I WILL

Make a request that will give me control over some aspect of my life.

LONELINESS

"I FEEL AS THOUGH I'VE BEEN SENTENCED TO SUCH LONELINESS," SAID NATALIE.

"ANYTHING YOU DO DEEPLY IS VERY LONELY," SAID KATAGIRI ROSHI.

"ARE YOU LONELY?" SHE ASKED.

"OF COURSE," HE ANSWERED, "BUT I DO NOT LET IT TOSS ME AWAY. IT IS JUST LONELINESS."

—NATALIE GOLDBERG

Victor was alone on the oncology floor. Well, not really alone. There were plenty of medical staff coming and going, and plenty of patients and their visitors spread among the rooms in the circle around the nurses' station. Victor even had a roommate, an amiable man, who was in the hospital for the first time in his life. But as far as Victor could determine in his own mental and physical confusion, he was the only one on the floor without visitors, either family or friends. Well, sure, the hospital chaplain stopped by once in a while. And there was the hospital social worker who'd come in about his mounting bills. Last week, he'd asked the nurse to phone his lawyer, and he'd actually looked forward to that visit, even though the pain had been especially bad that day. But today the loneliness was almost more than he could bear. It had never mattered much before; he'd been shy and reclusive all his life. But now, it was different; it looked as though he'd never leave this bed. Not for the first time, he wished he'd married, or at least had some family member who could be here with him. He heard laughter in the next room and the soft voices of his roommate and wife beyond the curtain. Victor closed his eyes and wished that it would all be over soon.

Twenty-nine-year-old Amy, a few doors down from Victor, had lots of visitors. Amy had always been a social gad-about, enjoying the company of the people she worked with at Natch Communications and the members at the church and club she'd recently joined. Her co-workers and college friends visited often, and her parents or her two brothers were a constant fixture in her room. A lighthearted banter and an upbeat positive spirit pervaded the room, urging her to laugh, get dressed, get well every day. Amy tried to keep up with it all, but in the night, when she was finally alone, she was less than positive; she was terrified. And she felt incredible loneliness. No one talked to her with any degree of seriousness about her situation. Though she lived on the oncology floor, though she could still feel the pain of the surgery, though she thought about ovarian cancer every single hour, no one close to her seemed to acknowledge it. Ignoring the dire possibilities was like ignoring a proverbial white elephant in her bed.

Combating loneliness, whether our situation is more like that of Victor or Amy, is a tremendous struggle. Facing our own death is one of the few things we have to do entirely on our own. Yet experts on death and dying have noted that several major factors can enable people to more peacefully face the possible end of their lives: a personal relationship, an atmosphere of open awareness, and a belief system that provides meaning. A close, fulfilling relationship with just one other person is crucial in combating the loneliness and the feelings of abandonment that are so prevalent at this time. So what does a person do when there is no family member or friend to confide in?

A health care provider, such as a physician or nurse or hospice worker, a spiritual leader, or even a volunteer-stranger might be the one to fill that role. Not one of these individuals carry the baggage that comes along with parents, family, or friends. Secrets, old wounds, expectations, guilt, fears, disappointments—none of these pieces is attached to strangers, medical workers, or chaplains. Seek out help; ask for a support person or a counselor from the inside or outside world.

If there is no one to talk with at a time when you really need someone, then think about the Psalms, which suggest casting our burdens on the Lord, how ever we imagine him to be. A talk with God—the light, the universe, the angels—will help unload the fears and worries. If our minds and hands are able, we can use a pen and notebook to further unload the mind and dispel some of the loneliness of the long days and nights. It takes only one conversation of substance to begin turning loneliness around.

PRAYER

Great Healer, have compassion on me. Walk with me. Talk with me. Present your listening ear and your thoughtful heart, if not directly, then through another person. Guide that person toward me and help me to recognize the presence of an earthly angel. Make me open my mouth and entrust that person with my thoughts. Amen.

QUESTION TO PONDER

Is my timidity keeping me from speaking up?

TODAY I WILL

Try to be honest about one of my worries with one other person.

DYING ALONE

NO ONE DIES ALONE.

EVERYONE IS BLESSED AND GUIDED.

—ELISABETH KÜBLER-ROSS

Diane always said it wasn't exactly the dying she was afraid of. She felt certain the hospice that cared for her would control any physical discomfort she might experience. Her nurses and doctors tried to answer specific medical questions she asked. The chaplain addressed her spiritual concerns. The social worker helped with insurance and family issues. But nagging always at the back of Diane's mind was her concern of dying alone. She wondered about her own impending death and who would be there for her.

Some believe that a God-given promise lies in the blessing of the permanence of the soul after death. Diane's family promised they would be there. They prayed for a peaceful death for their mother and grandmother. And indeed, Diane's children would call their mother's death "almost miraculous."

Diane had lapsed into a semiconscious state by noon on the day she died. She rested quietly, her breathing alternating between shallow and deep, noisy and quiet. She looked relaxed and comfortable; her skin was pale and cool. The nurses checked her often and medicated her for pain. Her family sat around the bed, reminiscing, laughing, and crying. They talked to Diane and to one another. As is often the case, Diane no longer acknowledged their presence. But they believed Diane could still hear them. They stroked her face and told her they loved her.

Then it happened. As her daughter leaned across the bed to smooth the pillow, Diane suddenly opened her eyes and gazed longingly at the foot of her bed. No one was standing there. At least, no one the family could see. The dazzling smile that crossed Diane's face was something they all talked about for a long time after her death. She reached out her arms, whispered, "Johnnie!" and took her last breath. Johnnie, her husband, had died twelve years earlier. Her family would swear he came to take her home.

There are truths and comforts for all of us who fear dying alone. Elisabeth Kübler-Ross says we are "blessed and guided." We may choose to believe it was Johnnie who was there for Diane. And right beside Johnnie was the God Diane believed in, and behind him, other friends and family Diane loved, who had also died. True, her living family was beside her, too. And perhaps Diane will be there for them someday, smiling that dazzling smile and extending her own hand in love.

PRAYER

O God, help me to take comfort in the permanence of my own spirit. Stay close to my side and guide me all the days of my life. When death comes, grant me the wisdom to wait quietly for loved ones and for you, Lord, to lead me safely home.

QUESTION TO PONDER

How can I be afraid if God and my loved ones are with me?

TODAY I WILL

Visualize God and those loved ones who have gone before me encircling me with their love.

DARK NIGHTS

INTO THE WOODS, IT'S TIME TO GO. I HATE TO LEAVE, I

HAVE TO, THOUGH. INTO THE WOODS; IT'S TIME AND

SO, I MUST BEGIN MY JOURNEY.

—STEPHEN SONDHEIM & JAMES LAPINE

There's nothing as long and lonely as the late hours on either side of midnight and the early hours before dawn, when the body and mind are in conflict: one wanting to sleep and the other allowing no such thing. Nothing is as frustrating as knowing one's body and mind need rest—and even more so one's spirit and emotions—and then not being able to shut them down. A barrage of thoughts, anxieties, and fears torment us during these hours.

"Years ago, everything seemed clear," writes John Tully Carmody, as he carries on a lengthy dialogue with God during his final days, "now I know nothing for certain. All around me and in me is dark. Now I'm readier for the problems of midnight, the ones requiring strength of soul."

That uncertainty about life—about what's happening to us, about how this disease is going to play out and what we'll be left with at the end, about how those we love will carry on—all this uncertainty increases our anxiety . . . especially at night, in the dark, when we're alone, when there are no more distractions to take our attention. It's in these dark hours that we're finally forced to look at what haunts and torments us. It's at these times that we finally begin to understand that old line "the dark night of the soul."

But we can step back and remember that these particular nights aren't the only times in our lives when we've lain awake, sleep a long way from our grasp. Not many of us get by in this life without having to go into the dark woods, where there are no maps or blueprints, where one's old habits and roles no longer work. There have been other times in our past when the path has been not only unfamiliar but scary. And yet we struggled through them and now they're memories, distant realities.

And therein may be the secret to getting through dark times. We must remember what we did, how we did it, what we drew on. Our disease cannot invade the soul, it cannot suppress memories, it cannot shatter hope, it cannot steal courage, it cannot kill the love of those around us. We can still draw on these strengths. They are the essence of who we really are . . . not this disease. So, as we lie in the darkness, we can try to face our anxiety head-on. The age-old prayer in Psalms says "though I walk *through* the valley of the shadow of death" (KJV). In order to get to the other side, we *must* walk through the shadows, those woods, that valley. Of course, that's easier said than done. Emily Dickinson knew that when she wrote: "The bravest grope a little, and sometimes hit a tree, directly in the forehead, but as they learn to see, either the darkness alters, or something in the sight adjusts itself to midnight and life steps almost straight."

"Would you sit through the night with me?" my mother asked, ever so hesitantly. Of course I would. And so would others. Ask for a hand to hold, a warm body in the chair next to your bed. If you wish, talk about your fears, worries, anxieties, but sometimes all you really want is a presence nearby, to give some light to the night as you work through your own personal woods.

Believe it or not, there will come a time when you'll prefer not to talk at all. You'll withdraw from the world around you. In *Gone From My Sight*, Barbara Karnes describes it as separating from the outside and going inside, where there is a sorting out, an evaluating. "On the inside," she says, "there is only room for one. It's a processing that's usually done with the eyes closed. Sleep increases. Although it appears to be just sleep to outsiders, it's actually important work that is going on inside on a level of which others aren't aware."

And so it may be that in these vertical, eyes-closed times that "We grow accustomed to the dark, when light is put away, as when the neighbor holds the lamp to witness her goodbye. A moment when we uncertain step for newness of the night. Then fit our vision to the dark and meet the road, erect." (Emily Dickinson)

PRAYER

Protector and Comforter, help me through this night, where all around me and in me is dark. Help me find the courage to face my fears about this journey. Walk with me and talk with me and give me your hand. Help me through this deep valley, these dark woods, so that I will come out on the other side, stronger and at peace. Amen.

QUESTION TO PONDER

What do I fear in the late, lonely hours of darkness?

TODAY I WILL

Pull one of my fears out of the darkness and examine it in the light.

WORDS

AT THE END OF ONE'S LIFE, WORDS LOSE THEIR IMPOR-

TANCE; TOUCH AND WORDLESSNESS TAKE ON MORE

MEANING.

—BARBARA KARNES

"Get well soon!" proclaim the cards we receive in the mail or the visitors who leave our rooms. "You'll be better in no time!" encourages another who doesn't want to be the bearer of anything but positive words. "I'll see you next week," says the regular visitor. "Stay well."

Stay well? Get well soon? You'll get better? Don't these people have a clue? This isn't a broken leg we're dealing with. As one man put it, "I'm *not* going to get better, soon or ever." The visitors and card senders mean well and probably are groping for something comforting to say, but it's often painful to hear these words.

Adrienne sat in an examining room, waiting for her oncologist. She was nervous and felt less than dignified in the skimpy, blue-and-white cotton hospital gown. The calendar on the wall reminded her that she and her doctor would soon be planning out her next round of chemotherapy sessions. Next door she overheard a man yell, "Don't call me Larry! You have no right! My name is Mr. Grayson! Lawrence Grayson!" Adrienne checked the mirror to see if she looked healthy . . . to see if she looked like a regular person. She understood the man's anger, his fight for control over the shreds of dignity remaining as a cancer patient. She understood what it was like to be stripped of everything but the terror. "The doctors and nurses can pump us full of chemicals," she said, "strip us naked in their offices, and call us Larry or hon or dear. But our souls . . . we own our souls."

The words her friends, relatives, and medical staff used with her sometimes made all the difference between a good day and a bad day.

Sticks and stones may break my bones, but words will never hurt me. That old children's chant is wrong and everyone knows it. Words do hurt. Words don't have to be intentionally harmful to bring pain; they can be honest instead: "I'm sorry to tell you that you have a tumor." Words don't have to be mean-spirited to cause pain; they can be false instead: "I read that cancer might be the result of anger. What are you angry about, dear?" Some words are huge and are delivered in a heartbeat, such as: "The prognosis is not good; a few days to two weeks at the most." Some are cushioned in the midst of conversation: "You've lost another hunk of hair, dear." Some are like a slap: "Well, you've been smoking your lungs out for years; it's no wonder you've gotten yourself in this condition!" Others are served up on the side: "Is this a new lesion, Mr. Miller?" Others are small and given over and over: "Get well soon. Get well soon." Words can be scary, even terrifying; they can be painful, even debilitating.

What do we do with the words that float through our lives and become part of our night sweats? What do we do when painful words shape our days and make our long nights longer? Adrienne uses imagery. She says that she thinks of herself as part of a tribe of warriors fighting for a prize dearer than any piece of land, more important than any religious dogma.

Others use humor and honesty. An obviously ill man recently brought his empty pill bottle in to the local pharmacist. He smiled and said, "Listen, I want just half an order. I probably won't be around long enough to use the whole bottle. Might as well save a few bucks while I can."

Sometimes it helps to share words with those fighting the same or a similar battle. This might come in the form of a support group or just one other person who's experiencing some of the same thoughts and feelings, aches and pains. Adrienne seeks out other cancer patients. She feels like they're in a secret society together, and that they'd recognize each other anywhere, even as complete strangers out on the street.

Words and pronouncements may become less painful the longer we live with them. If the words are wrong or dishonest, we can examine them and throw them away or let them slide in one ear and out the other. If the words are honest, we can analyze them and eventually take them on like a new vocabulary list. We can use our own words to help others understand what we're feeling, thinking, and learning. Above all, it helps to know that those visitors and card-givers are awkwardly fumbling for a way to talk to us in our strange new worlds. Their befuddled words are merely words and not always the best expression for what's going on in their hearts.

PRAYER

Lord, help me gather the words of the day and sort through them. Help me toss them away, keep them for further study, or treasure them in my heart. Help me discern the motive of the wordgivers so that I can better understand their words. Grant me the patience and willingness to help others talk with me so that our visits together are meaningful and helpful. Amen.

QUESTION TO PONDER

What words spoken to me today made me feel respected?

TODAY I WILL

Sort out the kinds of words that are useful to me, and those that are not. I'll tell someone what I learned.

ANGELS

THE VERY PRESENCE OF AN ANGEL IS A COMMUNICA-
TION. EVEN WHEN AN ANGEL CROSSES OUR PATH IN
SILENCE, GOD HAS SAID, "I AM HERE. I AM PRESENT IN
YOUR LIFE."

—TOBIAS PALMER

Angels are more popular than ever. Angels, defined in their purest form, are messengers sent by God to help us. Angels can be seen or unseen; they can be actual people in our lives or simple events that leave us shaking our heads in wonder. Everyone, it seems, has an angel story to tell. Phyllis's angel story involved a bare lilac branch and her own fear and discouragement in facing upcoming cancer treatments.

"It was March, and the kids wanted an Easter egg tree," Phyllis explained. "Easter was the furthest thing from my mind. I was worried about chemotherapy and my newly diagnosed breast cancer. But, like children, they begged and insisted, so a few weeks before Easter I broke off a good-sized branch from a dead-looking bush in our neighborhood. I took it home, spray painted it white, and stuck it in a coffee can filled with plaster of paris. When the base had hardened, the kids and I decorated the can and hung dyed eggs with colored ribbons from the starkly barren branches. The Easter egg tree sat on the kitchen table, its bare limbs reminding me of my own personal winter. It seemed spring and recovery were a long time away." Several weeks passed. Phyllis experienced the discomforts and side effects she had dreaded from her cancer treatments. Her hopes of ever feeling well again were diminished. Phyllis longed for a sign of spring and a promise of her own recovery.

Elizabeth Barrett Browning said "Earth is crammed with heaven. And every common bush afire with God." Phyllis would tend to agree, because the week before Easter, she received her communication of hope from God from a very common-looking branch. Dead as the Easter tree had appeared for so many weeks, during the week before Easter, tiny buds began to appear on its white painted branches. Phyllis watched in amazement as every day, the brittle branch submerged in a solid base of plaster brought forth more leaves and finally plump purple blossoms. By Easter Sunday, that dead-looking branch was in full bloom—fragrant lavender, brilliant green, and appearing very much alive on the kitchen table. Was the lilac tree her own angel messenger sent to comfort and encourage her? Or were her children the angels, insisting she remain rooted in the activities of their family traditions and her own everyday life? Phyllis and her family took it as a sign of hope and the presence of God during a trying time in their lives.

So angels are with us as commanded by God, ministering spirits who help us in times of need. Perhaps they come in the gift of a gentle caregiver or kind neighbor; in the miracle of a blossoming branch or a stranger who offers you comfort in a hospital waiting room; or even from your own family, who reaches out to you with a hundred different loving gestures. The first step in recognizing your own ministering angels is to be open to them. Just as Phyllis recognized the lilac blossoms as a sign from God, so can our own personal miracles be considered communication from God. Those signs should serve as a hopeful message that even in our darkest winters, God and his angels are present in our lives.

PRAYER

God, help me to be aware of the presence of angels in my life. Allow me to recognize even silence as a message from you. Keep me open to miracles that draw me closer to you. Grant me hope because of their presence. Amen.

QUESTION TO PONDER

Who or what in the past few days has been my ministering angel?

TODAY I WILL

Think about my most recent miraculous encounter and tell someone how it brought God closer to me.

WHY ME?

DIE EVERY DAY. BE REBORN AGAIN EVERY DAY.

—NIKOS KAZANTZAKIS

Audrey couldn't believe she had cancer. How could she possibly have cancer and be pregnant, too? She was healthy and had followed a strict vegetarian and whole-grain diet so she wouldn't end up like her grandmother, who had died after childbirth with complications from kidney cancer. In the end, would she be just like her? Audrey wanted to get up and breathe deeply, but her lungs hurt. Everything hurt. She'd heard a nurse say that too much fluid was building up, that she weighed thirty-five pounds more now than she did a month ago. She couldn't be that sick. She couldn't be dying—not with a baby coming. But she felt so strange. Everyone seemed worried; she was worried, too. When she looked in a mirror, she didn't recognize herself. Why did they close the door every time they left the room? Why did they whisper? She didn't like being alone. She couldn't die. She had too much to do. She *knew* she was supposed to be this baby's mother. If she died, who could love those she loved the way she did? She had to tell someone, but she was too tired. She couldn't talk. She felt sick . . . but dying?

Disbelief in a doctor's diagnosis of our bodies. Disbelief that we could actually be dying. How could something so damaging be happening, especially when we've followed all the rules, especially when we're in the midst of creating something good—a baby, a family, a career, a book, an important project? How can lives of promise be so completely undermined by disease?

Larry Dossey in *Healing Words* provides plenty of examples that serious illness strikes with no quotient of fairness. Saint Bernadette, who in 1858 saw the vision of the Virgin at Lourdes where thousands of healings are said to have occurred, didn't receive such a healing; she died of bone cancer at the age of thirty-five. Sri Ramana Maharishi, the most beloved saint of modern India, died of stomach cancer. Highly evolved spiritual leaders get just as sick as atheists. Highly skilled and knowledgeable medical practitioners get just as sick as the patients they treat. On the other side of the coin, plenty of people break all the rules of good health and live to be ninety.

Our bodies are subject to genetic diseases and prone to infections. "Bodies have minds of their own, which do not always accurately represent our psychological and spiritual understanding. Our bodies can act up, break down, and get sick without ever consulting us," says Dr. Dossey. Although we might accept cancer in our cat or dog as nature's way, we don't accept our own disease so naturally. We torment ourselves with the why and the how and the should-haves and the unfairness of it all. The simple truth is that we don't know why serious illness develops in some people and not in others; until we know more, it's a fact of life on this earth.

Audrey's pregnancy ended. While she was *thinking* about dying, her baby did. In disbelief and in grief, she said, "That's how it is . . . sometimes death occurs and nobody feels it—not even me." Left with a tremendous amount of physical and emotional pain to sort through, Audrey physically recovered and, oddly, with no trace of cancer. Yet, as anyone who's ever walked that tenuous line between life and death would understand, she takes each day as it comes, knowing that in one doctor's visit, she could be on the other side again. She no longer feels invincible. She has learned that her body has a mind of its own.

And doesn't that single fact remind us to live every day as fully as we can, as deliberately and positively as we can—even if we're confined to a small space or to a limited time? That single fact reminds us to stop wasting our time trying to figure out why we were given this dire diagnosis, and instead try to focus on how to live out our days more completely.

PRAYER

Dear God, help me realize this disease didn't creep into my body as a punishment for the things I did or failed to do. Remind me that illness doesn't have to take over my mind, my heart, and my spirit, too. Lift me from despair and fill me with hope for a new day. Amen.

QUESTION TO PONDER

Do I blame myself for my illness?

TODAY I WILL

Look in the mirror of my heart and know that I'm still there in that reflection.

ANGER

SHE LOVED LIFE. I DON'T THINK SHE EVER CAME TO
TERMS WITH THE FACT SHE HAD TO DIE. I THANK HER
FOR THAT. SHE SHOWED ME THE STRENGTH AND
DETERMINATION I'D WANT IF I HAD TO FACE SOME-
THING LIKE THAT. RIGHT UP TO THE END SHE WAS STILL
MAD SHE HAD TO GO.

—ART CHAPMAN

When we lose, we are angry. Why me? Why
now? It's not fair . . . why? Anger is such a large part of any
serious illness. More than just a "stage" in the steps toward
our own understanding, it is a feeling that completes the
picture of our emotional makeup. Anger, like other emotions, can energize. Anger, well directed, is a healthy and
expected response. Sometimes, however, we need permission to admit we're angry.

So who's angry? Of course, the answer is "Me! I'm dying
and I'm furious about it! I stand to lose everything." Like
the anger of a young mother who is fighting mad because
she must leave her family, your anger may strengthen your
resolve to use every day to its fullest; to savor the moments
with family; to love your loved ones with a fierceness born
of that anger. Some would call that determination or fight
or a passionate will to live. Anger, in its positive form, can
transform us.

Who else is angry? Your loved ones may be. A teenage
girl in a support group cried openly and said, "I'm angry at
God because he took my father." Others may be angry at
you for getting sick. It makes no sense, but anger directed

at the one who is ill is a real aspect of how caregivers and families often deal with letting go. "How can you leave me?" a husband asks of his dying wife. Sometimes, children may not understand and may turn away from us. Teenagers slam doors and retreat to their rooms. Or you may be angry at medicine in general and at the doctors or nurses for being unable to save you. Anger can be expressed verbally, with shouting, crying, questioning. Or it may be repressed with hostility, depression, sarcasm, or bitterness. Like all feelings, anger in itself isn't bad, but necessary. It's part of healing. What's important is that you learn to express it without hurting yourself or someone else.

A man named Orville Kelly in Kansas City, Kansas, founded an organization called Make Today Count to help those with cancer and other life-threatening diseases cope in a positive way. By the time he died in 1980, he had touched the lives of thousands of cancer patients, their families, and caregivers with his nationally known support group. While he battled his disease, he and his wife spoke publicly, conducted seminars, and were featured in hundreds of publications. One of their goals was to promote open and honest communication when dealing with a terminal illness. They strove to improve quality of life with increased professional and community awareness of the needs of the terminally ill. Make Today Count wanted to help those with life-threatening illnesses make each day something worthwhile and special. Orville suspected he would not survive, and yet he was very upbeat, encouraging honest conversation in dealing with feelings.

Can you talk about your anger honestly with someone you trust? Can you express it openly by pounding on a pillow or a punching bag? Write down your feelings or use art to express them with crayons or paint. Cry and rant, then channel the anger to something concrete and positive. It's okay to be angry, and expressing it can free you from it. Maybe you will be like the young woman who "loved life . . . and was mad she had to go." Her honest approach left her husband thanking and remembering her for that.

PRAYER

Dear God, some days, I am so angry. I love life, and I don't want to leave my loved ones. Help me to express my anger in ways that are healing for me and my family. Bring me the comfort that comes from knowing I have directed all my emotions toward an appreciation of my life today. Amen.

QUESTION TO PONDER

What are the ways I can express my anger today? How can my loved ones redirect their anger toward positive outcomes?

TODAY I WILL

Name one thing I am angry about and identify how I can express my anger positively.

DISAPPOINTMENT

PUT AWAY FROM YOU ALL BITTERNESS AND WRATH AND
ANGER AND WRANGLING AND SLANDER, TOGETHER
WITH ALL MALICE, AND BE KIND TO ONE ANOTHER,
TENDERHEARTED, FORGIVING ONE ANOTHER. . . .

—EPHESIANS 4:31-32 (NRSV)

Diabetes had taken a toll on Eve's health over the years. Her kidneys were failing, as were her eyesight and her ability to walk. She'd once been athletic, talented, and creative, an independent, hardworking woman, someone fun to be around. Then her health began to fail. She tried to immerse herself in smaller projects, but soon even those were too much. She couldn't believe that her body was breaking down in slow motion. Her husband promised that he'd take care of her and never put her in a nursing home. But he died unexpectedly. She couldn't live alone in their house. Her medical needs were great, and her children couldn't take care of her in their homes. Depression, resentment, and disappointment moved into the nursing home with her. Eve had a difficult time talking with or even being civil to her children.

Jessie's life was similar to Eve's. A once vibrant and busy woman—the child of homesteaders—she ended her years confined to her house, and then to her bed. She resigned herself to the diagnosis of untreatable cancer; the disease that had also claimed her parents, two siblings, and her husband. She knew it would get her, too. Along with the diagnosis and the resignation came resentment. She'd taken care of those in her family who had succumbed to cancer, so now her family could take care of her. But although her daughter loved her and went out of her way every day for her, Jessie sensed her innate repulsion to nursing procedures. Jessie grew increasingly disappointed in her daughter and let her know in many small ways.

Both Eve and Jessie had counted on a specific quality of life for their final years. But numerous expectations were lost along the way. They had to continually adapt, and change was not easy for them. Short on coping skills from the onset, their personal crises only added to that weakness. Personality changes seeped in as Eve and Jessie moved from being competent, vital women to dependent, resentful women.

Disappointment and change isn't easy on any of us. We can't claim a perfect set of coping skills. An irreversible, life-ending diagnosis can change the strongest of us into embittered people. For days on end, the smallest of courtesies, the least measure of kindness, the tiniest iota of humor, the weakest gesture of thoughtfulness may be too difficult to garner and give out.

How can we stop immersing ourselves in our disappointment and personal misery? Do we even want to try? Dr. Elizabeth Clark from the Albany Medical Center suggests that hope is a prerequisite for good coping. Eve and Jessie experienced broken hope. But it can be mended. "Broken hope," says Dr. Clark, "requires an adjustment of thinking. Each of us can choose to build a new hope or to create a substitute hope." Families cannot always be all things at all times; years of baggage can interfere.

If we want to share every detail of our last medical procedure, let's not unload on the first person we see. Instead, let's find someone who's interested: a medical caregiver or another patient who's traveled the same route. If we're disappointed in our children, let's unload it on a stranger, a close friend, or a spiritual counselor. If we wake up morning after morning feeling depressed and uncaring, let's ask for a professional counselor who can walk us away from some of the misery. If we can't find anyone appropriate with whom to share our frustrations, resentments, anger, and disappointments, let's give them to God, to the angels, to the universe. Bit by bit, let's unload it, and bit by bit we'll once again experience some of the hope, lightness, and love we once felt.

PRAYER

O God, help me diagnose my own spiritual and emotional dis-ease before I reject everyone I hold dear. Nudge me when I'm feeling resentful or disappointed or jealous of those who love and care about me. Help me gather gratitude and kindness for those times when they matter most. Amen.

QUESTION TO PONDER

Am I resentful of someone who visits me? How can I unload this resentment?

TODAY I WILL

Find a reason to be grateful for those I've been disappointed in and tell them.

UNRESOLVED ANGER

WILL HE BE ANGRY FOREVER,

WILL HE BE INDIGNANT TO THE END?

—JEREMIAH 3:5 (NRSV)

When speaking of her abusive ex-husband to her children, Andrea never called him anything other than "your father." In the thirty years since their divorce, Andrea had raised their five children by herself, working as a social-service secretary in an adoption agency. She loved her job and was good at it. Although she maintained a positive "go-get-em" attitude, as a single parent she couldn't resolve her anger about her ex-husband. Deep down, she was just furious with him. One day when she shared a comment about "your father" to her adult children, her daughter said, "Mom, maybe it's time to let go of your anger. That story is thirty-five years old, after all." Andrea sighed and agreed, but somehow it was easier said than done.

In the last year of her life, after Andrea had been diagnosed with untreatable cancer, her anger toward her ex-husband intensified, and its force seeped out around her. She knew she should forgive him, because her anger was affecting other relationships. Besides, it was such a heavy burden; she didn't want to die with all that darkness. But how was she going to exorcise it from her life? The anger was so deep.

Andrea's relationship with her ex-husband was unfinished business she had never resolved. Unresolved anger carried around for years, even to the end of one's life, is too heavy to carry alone. It must be sorted out piece by piece, analyzed, and thrown away. It's not an easy job, especially if the anger has been simmering for decades. Even Jesus knew that forgiveness and letting go were not easy tasks. He suggested that it could take seventy-seven times to finally realize forgiveness.

Request a counselor, a therapist, or a chaplain to talk to or visit with. That's a positive, and often courageous, first step. These trained people have skills and techniques to help us walk through our pain, step by step, little by little, until one day it's all gone. Unload it all: from your own weaknesses and errors and mismanagement to that of others. Forgiving ourselves for our mistakes is as important as forgiving another for his or hers. A trusted friend or family member could also be helpful, although expectations and shared history sometimes gets in the way. Ranting and raging on paper with a very black pen, then burning the papers as a symbol of letting them go, can also be healing.

Matthew, a systems analyst, handled his anger by both confronting and dodging it. To his caregiver, he admitted his personal anger about two regular visitors. "Please ask them not to come by again. I don't want to talk to them anymore." That's a powerful resolution. If someone trustworthy can run interference for you, then ask her or him to keep certain people out of your room. There's no better time. Peace and serenity are your goals, not anxiety and anger. Admit aloud your anger about a person from your past—even someone long dead. Get that relationship off your chest. Matthew did. He continued his anger-cleansing by talking about his father, a demanding, ego-centered man who'd died years earlier. He analyzed, sorted, sifted . . . and finally resolved his anger. A free spirit took its place.

Andrea finally started working through her anger, piece by piece. One day she cried for her ex-husband, for herself, for the lack of redemption between them, for the sadness of it all. Finally, his dark personality lifted from her heart—and, not unexpectedly, her own darkness, too. After her death, Andrea's daughter found slips of paper in her mother's makeup kit, in her coin purse, in her toothpaste drawer, in her kitchen drawer. They all said the same thing:

"Forgiving is remembering and moving on. For me to forgive is to make a conscious decision, with the help of God, to refuse to let anger control me any longer." Andrea had found a way to work out a new mindset for herself.

It's been said that there's only a thin line between hate and love. Some of that complexity was clear in both Andrea and Matthew. Deep anger is difficult to work through, but we must force ourselves to do it. The final reward is the start of a new life—no matter how short that life is—with a free spirit, a peaceful heart, and a readiness for what comes next.

PRAYER

Merciful God, help me sort through my life, recognizing the source of any anger that's stirring up my insides and causing me unrest. Help me find a way to let go of any bitterness that's sapping my strength. Give me the courage to admit and deal with old angers so I may have peace. Amen.

QUESTION TO PONDER

Am I angry with someone? Who?

TODAY I WILL

Recognize that it's okay to admit my anger and begin to resolve it.

DESPAIR

I WALKED A MILE WITH SORROW

AND NE'ER A WORD SAID SHE;

BUT OH, THE THINGS I LEARNED FROM HER

WHEN SORROW WALKED WITH ME.

—ROBERT BROWNING HAMILTON

Jack was extremely upset when he learned the "verdict," as he called it. He'd been sentenced to death by a jury of masked staff who didn't seem to realize that he'd only been around for two dozen years. He wasn't even going to be allowed to live long enough to prove to all those who didn't believe in him that he could be a success. Didn't they see their mistake? He was too young to die. Well okay, if that's the way they want it, if he was going to die, then he would do anything he darn well pleased. Why work? Why get out of bed? Why not eat steak, deep-fried shrimp, and pecan pie every day? Why not get high on drugs?

A death sentence, without the chance of parole or remission, without the opportunity of a pardon or a cure, can bring such a black cloud of despair that one simply doesn't want to wake up in the morning. Suddenly, life no longer has value or meaning. A devastating verdict can very well leave one dead on the inside long before death occurs on the outside.

The tragedy of this kind of despair is that it can happen to any of us, whether we've been given the death sentence or not. Suddenly the very things we've always held aloft teeter and crash to the ground. *What's the use?* we think. Why not give up on everything we've believed in? It doesn't matter anymore anyway.

The truth is that we can't give up, because neither escape nor indulgence ever gave life meaning. And oh, this is the time of our lives when we need meaning the very most. Despair must be dealt with by facing the verdict squarely and dealing with it constructively. That means that in the face of deep personal crisis, like a fatal illness, one can still grow. How can dying contribute to growth? By our accepting it as an important and valuable part of life. Robert Herhold in *Learning to Die, Learning to Live* says: "It's too bad that dying is the last thing we do, because it can teach us so much about living." In other words, we might have received the death sentence, but we aren't dead yet.

In time, Jack realized that while this verdict meant he had a certain number of days left, even if he were cured, he'd still have only a certain number of days left. When he walked the hospital corridors, he saw others—even younger—with a similar verdict. Fairness, it seemed, wasn't part of the sentence. He finally concluded that maybe the quantity of his days wasn't as important as the quality of them. Photography, once just a pastime, now filled up his time. His morale improved; his days began to have value. One morning, he even said, "I'm hanging between happiness from what I'm learning about life and sadness that I have no future." And yet, Jack's photos had a future. They were concrete evidence of who the real Jack was, and they remained on the walls of the hospital and the homes of his friends and family long after he was gone. One of the profound differences between Jack's sense of future and that of other, healthier people is that Jack *knew* his days were numbered and he consciously chose to make them matter.

When sorrow walks with us, we must find ways to learn from her. Opening up our artistic side and allowing it to flourish is one way to make that happen. We can walk through the pain and anger, the sorrow and despair by making audiotapes or videotapes; taking photographs; writing poetry, essays, or journals; painting or drawing; doing handwork or carpentry; or sharing stories with others. One of these avenues will create a positive effect on our morale and will help us learn more about life and about ourselves in the process.

It's no small comment when Judy Tatelbaum writes in *The Courage to Grieve*, "Just as whole forests burn to the ground and eventually grow anew, just as spring follows winter, so it is nature's way that through it all, whatever we suffer, we can keep on growing." The New Testament's book of Romans says it, too: "Suffering produces endurance, and endurance produces character, and character produces hope, and hope does not disappoint us" (Romans 5:3-5, NRSV).

PRAYER

God of life, if I'm honest about my past—before this disease became part of my life—I see unexamined and unappreciated days. Help me realize that my remaining days may be the most important ones of my life. Show me how to walk with this dark sorrow and learn from her. Amen.

QUESTION TO PONDER

How might I move through despair and into new life?

TODAY I WILL

Decide on one way to express myself artistically.

GRIEF

LOVE, ANGER, FEAR, FRUSTRATION, LONELINESS, AND
GUILT ARE ALL PART OF GRIEF. IT IS IMPORTANT TO
UNDERSTAND THAT GRIEF IS NOT A SIGN OF WEAKNESS
OR LACK OF FAITH. GRIEF IS THE PRICE WE PAY FOR
LOVE.

—DARCIE SIMS

Ten-year-old Josh held up his crayon draw-
ing and said, "This is the grief monster who's gobbled up all
my good feelings." And we believed him. The picture was
all black and red, a roaring dragon with flaming hair and a
screaming mouth. It was a perfect way for this grieving child
to express himself and the experiences he couldn't quite
talk about yet. His twin sister had died just one month
before and he was angry. He was also confused, afraid, and
very sad. In the course of time Josh spent in the children's
grief group he attended, he learned that his grief could not
be "fixed." Rather, he learned that if he shared his thoughts
with those who were willing to listen, his grief monster
could be quieted and some of his good feelings could be
restored.

Grief is explained as the feelings we have when we lose
someone or something. When someone we love dies, we
feel sadness, loneliness, anger, emptiness. It seems a very
large grief monster has gobbled up our good feelings of joy,
security, or hopefulness. When we move, we may grieve the
loss of friendships, a home we love, a way of life. When we
are seriously ill, that grief monster may come to gobble up
our good feelings, leaving us feeling empty and alone.

Because a prolonged illness may rob us of our independence, our lifestyle, or even our view of the future, it is inevitable and even healthy that we grieve our losses. How we confront our own particular grief monsters may be the key to how we eventually understand these losses, too.

In his grief support group, Josh discovered that feelings aren't good or bad; feelings just are. He learned to feel his feelings and share them with others. He expressed them in activities, such as art and music. Josh carried his anger to the playground and ran it out in a basketball game. Sometimes he carried his sadness to his mother, whom he trusted, and left his feelings with her for a while. Often, Joshua cried with his mother because she reminded him it was okay for boys to cry. Many times, she cried with him. Josh also learned that it's okay if sometimes his grief monster even left him for a while. "Even though my sister died," Josh said, "I learned it's okay if sometimes I'm happy."

Battling that grief monster is hard work. It takes energy and courage to be patient with yourself. Some days the job will be so overwhelming that you may feel discouraged. That's when it's alright to feel the sadness, write it down in a letter, or draw or paint a picture. Then one day, you'll discover a good feeling that you'd forgotten was there.

The grief monster eventually visits all of us. But our gobbled-up good feelings are still there, waiting for us to rediscover them in the most unexpected ways, like a friend coming to visit or a welcome letter or even good news in the midst of hopelessness. At that children's grief group, Josh's final picture of his grief showed a smiling, less angry and scary grief monster, laying helplessly on his back, with four crooked legs pointed skyward. Standing next to him was a small boy with an arm raised in victory, and a large red smile drawn firmly on his face.

PRAYER

Dear God, how I long to find a way to quiet the grief monster who's come to visit me. I grieve the loss of so many things. I'd give a lot for a good feeling now and then. Changes are happening in me and in those I love. Help me to be brave enough to face all my feelings and to express them in ways that are healthy and healing. Amen.

QUESTION TO PONDER

What losses am I grieving?

TODAY I WILL

Identify a feeling I am having and express it, either by sharing it with someone or by doing an activity that will help release it.

HUMOR

EVEN WHEN A PERSON IS DYING, YOU CAN REMIND
THEM THAT DAY BY DAY THEY ARE STILL LIVING, THAT
ONE IS EVEN ALLOWED TO HAVE A SENSE OF HUMOR,
TO BE ABLE TO SMILE AT SOME OF THE SILLINESS THAT
GOES ALONG WITH WHAT WE CALL LIFE.

—VICTOR COHN

Do you remember the song that goes . . .
"even tho' you're only make-believing, laugh! Clown!
Laugh!"? Can humor and laughter comfort us in the
midst of our sorrows? Sometimes we need permission to
let humor and light-heartedness heal us, even in the face
of such serious issues as death and dying, grief and
bereavement.

Kay was a hospice chaplain who fought her own long
battle with breast cancer. Each day while working, and in
the midst of her own chemotherapy and radiation, Kay
wore a different brightly colored head scarf. To many who
knew her, Kay's scarves became a trademark, symbolizing
the colorful living light that she carried within herself. During her treatments for cancer, Kay fulfilled a long-held
dream and took dancing lessons with her husband. She carried on with life in spite of her own illness, ministering to
others, laughing at her own jokes, and bringing joy to those
around her with her unabashed love of living each day.
Kay's husband, Richard, says of her upbeat presence, "It was
like she brought in the sunshine with her."

Kay's funeral reflected her joyful approach to life. Her
beautiful scarves were draped over the altar and railings in

the front of the church. And, because Kay believed in light as a healing source and loved candles, dozens of tiny flames flickered throughout her service, reminding everyone of her own brightness in the face of darkness and disease. In the hospital chapel where Kay so often ministered to others, one of her well-remembered colored scarves is carefully preserved under glass with an engraved inscription that reads in part: "Choose life always." With humor and grace and always in a spirit of service, Kay lived that philosophy.

Those with long-term illnesses would seem to have no reason to find humor in their situation. Yet I recall my own chronically ill father often making us laugh. Complications from heart disease had left his belly unusually bloated. When we drove long distances on family trips, he would unzip and unbutton his trousers in order to be more comfortable. My mother, sister, and I still laugh about the time we stopped at a crowded tourist attraction. We had been driving for many miles, and when my father stepped out of the car to stretch his legs, his pants fell to his ankles. Even though he was sick, he laughed louder than any of us. In many of my memories of my father and his illness, it is his sense of humor and ability to laugh even in the face of great suffering that I remember the most.

Norman Cousins suggests laughter can heal us; perhaps not always physically, but emotionally and even spiritually. Somehow, Charlie Chaplin or Chevy Chase movies sound like more appealing therapy than drugs. Sometimes we worry we might laugh until we cry; or as music therapist and author Deanna Edwards says . . . "break down, fall apart and go to pieces." Laughter and tears are closely related. Humor can facilitate our expressions of sorrow.

Jessica was ten years old and dying of cancer. A friend of Jessica's mother heard Jessica had suffered another relapse and was once again hospitalized. With a heavy heart, the friend purchased a brightly colored helium balloon, tied a tiny teddy bear to the end of the balloon's string, and began the long drive to the hospital to visit Jessica. It was a warm day, and, without thinking, she rolled down the back car window for a little air. When she got to the hospital, she realized Jessica's balloon and little bear had escaped through the open window. Heartsick, she went in to visit Jessica empty-handed. As she sadly explained what had happened, Jessica started to laugh. "That's a great story!" Jessica exclaimed, clapping her hands in glee. "Somewhere out there is a tiny bear, my bear, looking down, saying very quietly, 'Oh help . . . somebody, help!'" Jessica's lesson was that even in the face of her own dying, living was what was important and, sometimes, that living could still be as silly as the image of a lost little bear tied to a floating balloon.

PRAYER

Creator, help me to look for some silliness in my life. Bring a smile to my face and to those who surround me. Give me the gift of lightheartedness as rest from the weariness of struggle. Offer me times of laughter and allow me to share them with others. Amen.

QUESTION TO PONDER

What has happened to me or someone else recently that might be considered silly or funny?

TODAY I WILL

Laugh at least once.

PAIN

YOU ARE BECOMING A FRIEND OF PAIN: WALKING
WITH IT, ALLOWING ITS ENERGY TO COME FORTH AND
MAKE YOU STRONGER. BLESSED ARE YOU.

—JANICE WELLE, O.S.F.

Joan Broysenko, in her book *Fire in the Soul*, writes about pain: "The great teachers of all traditions tell us not to pray for the cessation of pain but for the courage to endure whatever suffering we must traverse on the way to freedom." Certainly, in both chronic and acute illness, pain may be a part of the experience. How can we walk with it, draw energy from it, or allow it to make us stronger? Can pain be a blessing? Can any good come of it? How can we endure pain and grow? Or is it even necessary to endure it?

Pastor Bill's five-year battle with cancer became an inspiration to his son, Cole, who ran a marathon race with his father's pain in mind. In spite of his own knee discomforts and with others urging him to drop out, Cole ran and finished the race, saying, "I'm running this one for Dad. If he can stand the pain, so can I." Pastor Bill died shortly after his son's marathon, with the dignity of one who understood suffering as almost a spiritual cleansing. He was buried in the prize his son had won: a T-shirt that was worn under his clerical shirt and collar with the words, "Marathon Finisher" emblazoned across the front. Both father and son understood pain as part of the race and did not let it distract them from the task at hand. Bill's family says he finished what he started—a life lived with faith at its center—even when life's deepest pains threatened to overcome him.

With today's technologies, physical pain can be controlled in well over ninety percent of cases. Pain is not always inevitable, but there are many ways to treat it and still maintain alertness. Medications, administered orally or by injection, indwelling catheters or IVs, may offer relief. There are doctors and clinics who specialize in pain control. A specific focus for hospices is pain control.

Holistic techniques, such as music therapy, prayer, or meditation, may help to relieve chronic or even acute pain. Rachel Naomi Remen, M.D., in her book *Kitchen Table Wisdom: Stories That Heal* says we can learn from when "our mothers kissed our boo-boos to make them better. It doesn't help the pain, it helps the loneliness." Involving others in our pain with their touch and presence, through massage, biofeedback, or hypnosis, may be helpful. We shouldn't have to face our pain alone.

There are specific tools, such as printed charts called pain inventories, that allow you to document and assess your pain. This document helps you pinpoint where the pain is located, what it feels like, how long it lasts and what relieves it. The better able you are to describe your pain, the easier it will be for you to communicate your needs clearly to your caregivers and to gain relief.

There may also be other pain present, that of an emotional or spiritual nature. A trusted pastor or priest, rabbi, or counselor may help provide relief or healing. Again, prayer, meditation, education, and even just conversation may be helpful. Rabindranath Tagore said, "Let me not pray to be sheltered from dangers but to be fearless in facing them. Let me not beg for the stilling of my pain but for the heart to conquer it." It takes great courage to experience pain, and even greater courage to conquer it or grow from it. No one must endure pain needlessly. But, like Pastor Bill, you can experience the hardship of unrelieved pain and yet finish your race with dignity. And then, like him, as with many before, you will be blessed and energized.

PRAYER

Father, if pain is to be a part of my experience, then grant me the wisdom to understand it. Help me to express my needs to those who can help me gain comfort. Strengthen me as I walk with pain and bless me in the journey. Amen.

QUESTIONS TO PONDER

Have I told my doctors or nurses about my pain? Are there blessings to come from my experience with pain?

TODAY I WILL

Be strengthened by the knowledge of my own pain; keep a daily diary of my pain and what brings relief so that I can share the information with my caregivers.

WALKING

YOU SHOW ME THE PATH OF LIFE.

IN YOUR PRESENCE THERE IS FULLNESS OF JOY

IN YOUR RIGHT HAND ARE PLEASURES

FOR EVERMORE.

—PSALM 16:11 (NRSV)

Walking is a necessary part of any journey. It may be a short walk around the lake on a summer afternoon, or it may be the journey we call life that calls for the metaphorical walking in and out of our own daily experiences. The first, of course, requires we are physically able to walk. We'll need proper shoes and clothing and a destination. The second, however, we do symbolically every day, and it can be done purposefully, in our minds, as we walk through our present and past life experiences. We can still visualize pulling on our tennis shoes and fastening a leash to the dog's collar. But then, we can step forth, with imagery, into the woods or the open trail or the neighborhood sidewalk to cover the miles of life that stretch both in front of and behind us, without the physical restrictions of an actual walk.

As with any trail, the changes you see as you walk along are constant but sometimes subtle: a red berry on a bush that only yesterday appeared bare, a bird's nest exposed in the limbs of a tree whose leaves have fallen. In life, it may be an illness that disrupts your daily routine, or a celebration that has you skipping instead of walking. The landscape is always changing. Your walk may be enhanced by those changes or even challenged by it.

Have you ever walked into a cold, brisk wind and been

eager to finish and reach the warmth of home and the prospect of a hot cup of your favorite tea? You may have leaned into the wind, anticipating the destination and forgetting to be present to the moment. You notice your heartbeat accelerates and your breath comes harder. The more effort you put into your walk, however, the more physical benefits you may derive from it. Sometimes, life also brings that resistance. In our symbolic walk, facing adversity or even the prospect of our own deaths may make us more in tune with the richness of life around us. The effort may cause us to slow down, regain our strength, and shift our focus. Our leaning into the wind may then be replaced with a squaring of the shoulders and a determined, steady gait. We walk the path of life with our senses acutely aware of what surrounds us.

And what of a companion on our journey? Sometimes it feels good to walk alone. But often, having a person or God or even a favorite pet next to us makes it more of a blessing. We walk and talk and share our thoughts. We hold a hand, meditate, or pet an eager, furry head. We encourage one another. Journeys, especially strenuous ones, are easier when shared. A well-known expression says "Happiness shared is doubled, grief shared, halved." So it may be with your walk through the woods or the open trail or an illness. Even from the bedside you can experience the exhilaration of a simple journey, full of unexpected twists and turns and promises. Leave your tennis shoes behind. But bring a trusted companion and your own sense of wonder.

PRAYER

Dear God, come for a walk with me today. Guide me and comfort me as I discover what is beyond the next turn in my own journey. Help me to walk with confidence and awareness of the simple gifts that surround me. Give me strength to walk with a grateful heart. Amen.

QUESTION TO PONDER

Who will I take with me today on my walk? Where will we go?

TODAY I WILL

Make a list of five changes, either large or small, that I have noticed on my own life-walk this past month.

READINESS

HAVE NO REGRETS. RELINQUISH YOUR RESENTMENTS.

ALL YOU HAVE IS THE PRESENT MOMENT. BE STILL. BE

HERE. TRUST. ALL YOU HAVE IS NOW. IT IS ENOUGH.

—MELODY BEATTIE

Dying is such a strange, ethereal journey to undertake in the midst of living. Or perhaps—better said—living is such a strange undertaking in the midst of dying. When we no longer have a future as we've known it, the usual humdrum of life holds much less meaning. We're not as interested in renewing magazine subscriptions, listening to a sales pitch, changing the oil on the car, reading long, involved newspaper articles, or watching a TV series. At a certain point, things like seed catalogs, the investment club, or spring cleaning no longer motivate.

Ruth, a dying cancer patient, in Elizabeth Berg's novel *Talk Before Sleep*, says, "I find myself getting to this place of readiness. It's a kind of deep peace that I never felt before. And so, I lie there thinking, okay, I guess this is it, this is a good time, go ahead; and then the phone rings and it's somebody wanting to steam clean my wall-to-wall carpeting. And I want to say, 'Oh stop with this carpet nonsense. Listen to me. You've got to be careful. Say all you need to say, right away. You have no idea how fragile this all is!' But of course, all I say is, 'No, thank you.'"

When it comes to our dying days, we need to talk about and do the things that are important to us right now. There are days, of course, when we want business as usual. Well, as usual as it can possibly be. Joyce found herself sitting on the edge of the bathtub instructing her husband on how to bathe their son more gently. My father, Bob, often sat on the front steps admiring his blossoming apple trees, perhaps even smiling about the fact that he wouldn't have to harvest all those darn crabapples. My mother, Shirley, donned her sunglasses, wrapped up in a warm robe and rolled out on the hospital patio for iced tea. There she entertained friends as if nothing had changed. As for me, I'll make at least one last trip across the endless Dakota prairie so I can smell the sage and be the first to spot the antelope herds.

But as the days march on, there are more and more of the other kind of days, the kind where we need to settle things. To tidy up loose ends, common and uncommon. We might have questions that need professional answers. Friends and family need to know we've loved and appreciated them; some are struggling to tell us how much they love and will miss us.

Peter Noll, in *The Face of Death*, says that "since we live with death, we ought to think of it while living. To settle accounts, to draw a balance, is important and useful. The pastors should make it clear that it can be anyone's turn next; that everyone's turn comes at some point; that to prepare oneself is good; and that everything then might become quite easy." The bottom line? Let's say all we need to say, right away, because our lives are fleeting. Let's relinquish our resentments and try to have few regrets. Let's be as ready as we know how to be.

PRAYER

God, I seek peace. Help me accept that my time on this earth is limited. Give me the strength to say and do the things that need to be said and done. Give me the courage to step beyond what is comfortable and predictable to others. Help me live this day as though it were my last. And my first. Help me to be here right now and trust that it is enough. Amen.

QUESTION TO PONDER

Is there something I've been wanting to talk about?

TODAY I WILL

Make a specific request, one that's important to me.

DYING RIGHTS

PEOPLE DIE THE WAY THEY LIVE. THE WAY WE DIE IS AN INDIVIDUAL CHOICE. HELPING SOMEONE DIE MEANS ALLOWING THEM TO DO IT THEIR WAY. WE CAN DO IT OUR WAY WHEN IT IS OUR TURN.

—KAIROS

Care of the dying involves more than just symptom control. Donovan and Pierce, in *Cancer Care Nursing*, list the rights of the dying in their "Dying Person's Bill of Rights." It was written to ensure everyone at end-of-life would have the opportunity to know what their rights are while they are living until they die. Some of these one-line statements speak of the end-of-life dignity we all expect and deserve.

1. *I have the right to be treated as a living human being until I die.*
Ronald knew, above all else, that he wanted to die at home. Even though he had no primary caregiver to stay with him full time, his doctor found a hospice that arranged volunteer help that enabled him to remain in his tiny house. Ronald enjoyed his cats, meals in his own kitchen, and piano music provided by his friends. He lived with dignity and joy, as a "living human" in his own home until he died.

2. *I have the right to maintain a sense of hopefulness, however unchanging its focus may be.*
Julie thanks her doctor for never giving up on her. She describes him as a partner in her fight against her disease. She says, "He trusts me to believe in his care, to keep my body as healthy as possible, and to always have hope in my heart." Her hope changes but is always present. Its focus

may shift from hope for a cure, to freedom from pain, to an extended life. Hope is never static.

3. *I have the right to express my feelings and emotions about my approaching death in my own way.*
Lee was a stoic fellow who lived his life protecting and providing for his family. He was not comfortable speaking directly about his emotions or his impending death. He told his family he loved them but wished to avoid talking about his dying. They respected his wishes and did not judge his silence. They sat with Lee and held his hand.

4. *I have the right not to be deceived.*
Even those who work with dying children will tell you that the dying cannot be deceived—that they sense the truth and deserve to be told the facts in order to prepare for their deaths. Oftentimes, sharing the truth will help eliminate fear of unknowns that need to be discussed.

5. *I have the right to die in peace and dignity.*
There is no "right" place to die. If each of us had the luxury to choose, we would each choose differently. Mike wanted to go to his lake home. He was so ill, it seemed an almost impossible task. A loving nurse, who had become his friend, made arrangements for him with his doctor and a local hospice. Mike's last trip to his lake place was in an ambulance, accompanied by his wife and his nurse. He spent three glorious months enjoying the view of the lake from his window. Eventually, he died there, in the place most conducive for him.

6. *I have the right to be free from pain.*
Comfort is paramount on any journey: soft pillows, pleasant surroundings, a room with a view. So should it be on your final journey, and it is your right. You should travel as pain-free as possible and with your comfort goals clearly defined. If you need something to make you more comfortable, ask for it.

7. *I have the right to be cared for by caring, sensitive, knowledgeable people who will attempt to understand my needs and will be able to gain some satisfaction in helping me face my death.*

Lucy, a hospice nurse, spent many years working with the terminally ill. She expressed the thoughts of many caring, sensitive, and knowledgeable people who work with the dying when she said, "I treasure my years working as a hospice nurse. The work was intensely demanding, but also personally rewarding. My patients were my teachers and guides though some difficult lessons."

8. *I have the right to have help from and for my family in accepting my death.*

Fifteen-year-old Scott was desperate to be with his dying mother but didn't know what to say or do. His mother's nurses told him his mother could hear him, even if it appeared she couldn't. They encouraged him to sit by her bedside and talk to her. He was thrilled when she moved her eyebrows as he said he loved her. He would remember that gesture after her death and talk about it. It was her gift to him for being there.

9. *I have the right not to die alone.*

One gentleman chose to have his death be a celebration, surrounded by those he loved. Some choose to be sung to or stroked by loving hands or comforted with prayer. Ask those you love to stay with you so they will know your wishes.

10. *I have the right to expect that the sanctity of the human body will be respected after death.*

No one can know your wishes unless you state them. Talking about the difficult decisions while you are still able (for example, those regarding your body after death) may ease your mind and those of your loved ones. Ask for adequate information to make the best decisions for you.

AS I JOURNEY ON

PRAYER

O God, surround me with people who will allow me to live and die as I choose. Grant me wisdom to know what to ask for in order to achieve comfort and peace. Amen.

QUESTION TO PONDER

Are my rights as an individual being respected and granted?

TODAY I WILL

Name one personal right in my caregiving that could be improved upon; share that concern with my caregivers.

SOUL CARE

I WISH THAT LIFE NOT BE CHEAP, BUT SACRED,

I WISH THE DAY TO BE AS CENTURIES,

LOADED, FRAGRANT.

—RALPH WALDO EMERSON

Cheryl leans over the table in the early morning hour, her eyes drawn to the simple flickering flame of the candle burning in front of her. The tiny but powerful light opens her spirit to the possibilities of the day. In the evening, the flame calms her spirit for sleep.

Usually we hurry through our lives with bone-dry senses, unaware of the bluebell at our feet or a dog's rough tongue on our bare hand or the worried look on the face of the person across the hall or the taste of a freshly picked tomato or the sound of wind in the cottonwoods. Perhaps now—while we're more housebound or bedridden—we can take the time to indulge in the quiet, inexpensive riches around us. Just because we're seriously ill doesn't mean we've lost our creative spirit. The fact may be that our senses are actually heightened.

Thomas Moore in *Care of the Soul* suggests that all hospitals should have an art studio where patients could paint, sculpt, and move, with another room for patients to tell stories about their illnesses and hospitalizations. His idea was that the soul needs to speak by finding its own images. Everyone has an innate craving for beauty in some form. Cheryl's most frequent request was a wheelchair ride to the hospital lobby, where she could gaze at the fine art that graced the walls. For her, the art was medicine for her soul. But if we can't go to an art studio or a storytelling room, what can we do to open our senses more fully, to care for our souls?

The possibilities are as open-ended as our imagination. Think about sound and music. Why not keep a collection of Mozart's recordings near the bed, immersing ourselves in its inspired majesty whenever we choose? One woman requested that her son make a recording of his favorite poems. She could then listen to the voice of someone she loved and feed her soul at the same time, even at two o'clock in the morning. A trickling water fountain, a bubbling fish aquarium, a set of tiny bells, or a windchime bring soothing sounds into a room. What sound or whose voice, music, or words would you most like to hear?

Visual art, like photography, a piece of sculpture, or a personal collection of artifacts, feeds the soul in several ways. Somehow images like these calm our spirits, serving as reminders that order and genius and mystery are still a part of our worlds. One young man had a poster from his old room hung on his hospital wall; the one that showed a trim, fit skier skiing off a snowy cliff into a huge abyss of white space and silence. It seemed to give him the courage to face the daily barrage of tests and treatment he had to endure. Another man, a part-time potter, placed a diverse display of his art around his recliner. One pot contained a huge amaryllis bulb, just days from blooming; another held a leafy fern that thrived in the subdued light; smaller ones contained treats; one held fresh fruit; another kept his cards and letters in one place. Others stood empty, but full of an "earthiness" he wanted maintained in his room.

Sensitizing our imagination helps, too. Sometimes we've lit the candles, gazed our fill of faces and colors, listened to the day's final murmuring, and we're ready to sleep. But we can't sleep. Our bed may even feel like a cage. We want something to do while we're lying there. Joanne Williamsen, a hospice chaplain, suggested that we explore the spiritual images that are important to us. "Put a single image in our mind. Imagine God—or an angel or a person you've known—standing behind you, holding you." Place your head on your pillow, imagining it as God's shoulder. Close your eyes and imagine two "strong comforting arms around you, holding you close."

Go ahead and try it. Sink deep into the mattress and feel incredible support. Your back is leaning into God's chest. Be still and feel your hearts beating as one. God's voice is often found in the silence. Listen for the still, small voice and be comforted. Relax and let God hold you and carry you through the night.

PRAYER

Gentle Spirit, caress me with your loving touch. Open my eyes that I may see. Open my ears that I may hear. I want to sense your presence in all that's around me, in all that's available to me, in all that I'm still capable of enjoying. Help me live each moment until the last. Amen.

QUESTION TO PONDER

What does my soul crave?

TODAY I WILL

Care for my soul by requesting and enjoying something sensuous.

DANCE

Millie lived in a nursing home. She was elderly, had advanced diabetes and no family. Her mind was handicapped in some ways; her capacity to grasp concepts was limited. Millie was sharp in other ways—she always knew how long it had been between her pastor's visits. And she always wanted to share with him the latest important news, which to her meant those from the nursing home who had recently died. One day Millie grabbed Pastor Van by his shirt and pulled him close, as if to let him in on a big secret. "Nobody gets out of here alive," she whispered.

She was right, of course. Nobody gets out of life alive. At least in the context of what we call life on this earth. We all die, not just those of us with "terminal" or "fatal" diseases. The bigger reality is that life is fatal. Being born may very well be the most fatal thing we do. And neither doctors, nor statistics, nor even we ourselves can say how long we'll live. A parent may outlive a child. An ill patient may outlive his doctor. A middle-aged woman on dialysis may outlive a healthy athlete.

We've long been taught not to accept or talk about death, illness, and pain. In fact, our society goes out of its way to try to cure death, illness, and pain. By rushing through life doing our utmost to avoid negative, fatal, terminal things, we may be harming ourselves to an even greater degree. Struggle, illness, and crisis are some of our greatest teachers. Most of us know that at no time more than at a painful time do we live out of the depths of who we are. We become more aware of our need for each other and how powerlessness we are to save ourselves alone. It's during these times that most people look to a higher source of power. By looking at our lives and everything that happens in them as a process, we might actually be able to trust, even to dance.

How can a person dance when she has a fatal disease? Especially when she thinks nobody cares or wants to wait with her? Or when she herself is tired of waiting? A good number of spiritual leaders and medical experts have suggested that birth and death are merely doorways, and that the earth is our classroom. Elisabeth Kübler-Ross, an eminent expert on death and dying, maintains that "when we have passed the tests we were sent to earth to learn, we are allowed to graduate." So, if we're still waiting, as Millie waits in the nursing home, we can search for what is left to learn or to teach. Sometimes we don't even know if we're the student or the teacher. We're learning and teaching. And others are remembering what we did and what we said. Millie didn't know her pastor would remember, ponder, and share her comment for years to come. We learn. We teach. We graduate.

Kübler-Ross says that death allows us to "shed our body, which imprisons our soul the way a cocoon encloses the future butterfly, and when the time is right we can let go of it. Then we will be free of pain, free of fears, free of worries . . . free as a butterfly returning home to God . . . which is a place where we continue to grow and to sing and to dance. . . ."

> How can I learn to dance
> with a terminal illness?
> The moment that you ask that question
> the orchestra is already tuning up.
> Your willingness to explore is the dance.
> Your willingness to seek is the finding.
> The minute you say, "There's another way to do this,"
> you have found the other way.
> —*Emmanuel's Book II: The Choice for Love*

PRAYER

Lord of the Dance, how can you ask me to move—let alone dance—when life is being squeezed out of me like fat toes out of tight sandals? Help me to hear a melody. Help me, every so often, to feel rhythm in my fingers and toes. More than all this, loosen this burdensome sackcloth that weighs heavy on my spirit, and gird me with joy. Amen.

QUESTION TO PONDER

Today am I a student or a teacher?

TODAY I WILL

Say and believe—as the verse at left suggests—that there is another way to do this.

BODY CARE

OPEN YOUR MOUTH WIDE AND I WILL FILL IT . . . I
WOULD FEED YOU WITH THE FINEST OF THE WHEAT,
AND WITH HONEY FROM THE ROCK I WOULD SATISFY
YOU.

—PSALM 81:10, 16 (NRSV)

Hospitals are notorious for their bland diets, sterile environments, bright lights, and noisy corridors. Doctors order bed rest and their best potent drugs, but this medicine may be the opposite of what the patient actually needs. Whether we consciously know it or not, our traumatized bodies often crave that which is not readily available in the hospital, hospice, or sick room.

It's normal for the appetite to decrease. While the need for food diminishes, the desire for a few bites of specific foods often intensifies. Shirley craved the taste of fresh asparagus. Danny requested the heel of his mother's home-baked bread. Both patients could eat only a few bites, but their craving was satisfied. A chocolate shake from Dairy Queen may be more appealing than the hospital's Jell-O. Hot herbal tea with a slice of fresh lemon, or a glass of red wine, could whet the waning appetite. A trip to a restaurant, though exhausting, may do a lot to upgrade the appetite and the morale. Jog your taste buds. What would satisfy you?

If you're confined to a bed, you're probably aware of those "shampoo" products that dry clean your hair, without water. But nothing beats the feel of water on the skin. Warm sudsy water trickling down our backs is not only pleasurable, it brings solace and peace to our bodies and minds.

Though it may require much energy to get there, a bath or shower soothes the troubled soul, massages weak limbs, caresses the neck, hugs the shoulders, and kisses every nerve and follicle of a tired body. The running stream of water, with its gentle trickles and laps, sits easy on sound-weary ears and cluttered minds. The liquid warmth ripples and glides over touch-starved skin like silken underwear. Add herbal bath salts and a lightly scented shampoo, and the body is further restored.

Water massages skin, but so do fabrics and hands. Bed baths. Back rubs. Shoulder and neck rubs. And best of all, foot rubs. Add scented lotions and your pampered body might even yelp with delight. If you're in a hospital room, ask a relative to bring your own pillow, favorite blanket, quilt, or old soft robe from home. Fabrics not only give us warmth and familiarity, but they add warmth and color to our rooms. How about a softly lit lamp rather than the harsh overhead lights?

It's been proven over and over again that the furry, wiggling, licking touch of an animal can calm the body and tickle the heart. Adam was suffering from acute liver rejection in intensive care. Because of the toxins in his blood, he was psychotic, barely alert. An elderly golden retriever, calm and mature, stopped by for a visit. The nurse allowed him to climb up on a chair so Adam could see him. The dog licked his hand, and Adam became cognizant enough to recognize the dog and take some interest. Some patients have been known to bury their faces in a visiting dog's fur and laugh with delight. Anxious eyes and hearts become more hopeful and happier when pets visit.

Music therapy is another way of relieving stress and strain on the body. If you're at home, you can choose your own recordings or ask a friend to find the kind of music that relaxes and soothes. Some hospitals have music carts with a variety of musical recordings to choose from. Others sponsor musicians, like harpists, who visit the rooms of the very ill, calming the agitation of both patients and caregivers. The sound of those ethereal strings has been shown to lower blood pressure and blood sugar levels.

Sometimes the body doesn't need the protection and sequestering of a secured hospital room; sometimes it needs nature's elements. Adam got an extraordinary dose of medicine the day his sister wheeled him outside. There he felt the cool fog of the canyon on his skin and a touch of breeze that played with his blankets; he smelled the fresh air and found a cluster of white and purple iris to admire.

Let's ask for the taste of a fresh, ripe pear or the furry, wiggling touch of a friendly dog or the deep fragrance of purple lilacs or the caress of warm water on our skin. If need be, let's ask relatives or friends to run interference for us. It's almost a guarantee that they will jump at the chance to do something—anything—to help us, rather than sitting immobile and at a loss at our sides. Let's empower them to empower us.

PRAYER

My God, you're the only one besides me who knows the terrible disrepair of my body. I need your gentle prodding to help me discern what I could do today that would help me feel a measure of satisfaction, even pleasure. Give me the encouragement I need to make life-giving requests. Amen.

QUESTION TO PONDER

What does my body crave?

TODAY I WILL

Care for my body by requesting or enjoying something sensory.

HOSPICE

YOU MATTER BECAUSE YOU ARE YOU. YOU MATTER TO
THE LAST MOMENT OF YOUR LIFE, AND WE WILL DO
ALL WE CAN NOT ONLY TO HELP YOU DIE PEACEFULLY,
BUT ALSO TO LIVE UNTIL YOU DIE.

—DAME CICELY SAUNDERS

In an ideal world, we would talk openly and often about our views of end-of-life. We would wisely discuss with our families issues regarding our own, inevitable deaths. The topics would encompass not only living wills and estate planning, power of attorney, insurance, and provisions for survivors, but more personal subjects relating to our future wishes for terminal care, organ donations, and funeral arrangements. Unfortunately, however, in our society today, death is often a taboo subject, something we avoid talking about until it's too late. Then, when we are suddenly faced with the reality of a terminal illness or the death of a loved one, we are overwhelmed with how and where to begin.

There is hope for all of us in a philosophy-of-care called hospice. First established in England in the 1960s, today's modern hospice helps the terminally ill with expert pain control, more autonomy in their own care, family support, and an opportunity to really live until they die. Hospice can offer an alternative to living our last days in a hospital. Because hospice is not a place, it can function well in several settings. While most people experience hospice care in their homes, there are also hospice-designated beds in some hospitals and nursing homes, as well as free-standing hospice facilities scattered throughout the world. While to some a hospice referral is a surrender of hope, its experience for thousands, perhaps millions, of others has been quite the opposite. Today in the United States and Puerto Rico alone, there are approximately twenty-five hundred hospices. They offer a health care option for men, women, and children of all ages, races, and socio-economic standing, and for all kinds of terminal illnesses. Hospice offers the hope of living well until we die.

Edith wanted to go home. She had been in and out of the hospital for months. Her doctors continued tube feedings and medications designed for her comfort. However, with Edith's permission, further treatments to slow her progressive disease had been stopped. Edith was homesick and tired and missed the cozy basement apartment she shared with her sister. Her nurses noted she was depressed and withdrawn. A social worker suggested a hospice referral and her doctor agreed.

So Edith made the decision to go home, but not without much apprehension and many concerns. Would her care be compromised? How could she and her sister manage the dizzying array of treatment and medicine schedules? Would her doctor still follow her care? Who would provide for her medical needs at home? Who would pay for it?

Edith's first introduction to the concept of hospice came when she discovered her new caregivers had completely disassembled a hospital bed in order to pass it through a basement window and into her living room to set it up in the place she'd requested. Once settled comfortably among her belongings, with her calico cat at her feet and her sister at her side, Edith met her new hospice nurse and social worker. They asked her questions that helped her realize that she and her family were at the heart of this situation. Her nurses empowered Edith to make choices that would ensure quality medical care. Her symptoms would be managed at home as they had been in the hospital with her doctor in concert with other professionals offering physical, emotional, social, and spiritual support right there in her own home. They assured her that her comfort was paramount. Edith's nurses visited weekly at first. Later on, nursing visits were more frequent, and nurses were always available on call twenty-four hours a day. Edith's pastor visited, and well-trained volunteers came to help with meals, converse with Edith if she felt up to it, and gave Edith's family respites when they needed to get away for a few hours. A social worker offered assurances that when Edith died, they would continue to visit her sister, if she wished, in bereavement follow-up for at least a year. Edith relaxed and basked in the surroundings of home. Friends came and went at Edith's direction. She was comfortable and in control, and she was living her days surrounded by love and caring.

Hospice did nothing to hasten Edith's death, nor did they prevent it. She was home for three months before she died quietly, with her hospice nurse (who had become her friend), her sister, her pastor, and even her calico cat at her side. In the end, there were no tubes or needles, no machines or beeping monitors. Instead, in her own living room, there were family photographs, flowers, soft music, and loved ones surrounding her hospital bed. Edith died with dignity in the caring arms of hospice.

PRAYER

Is hospice an option for my care, God? Help me and my family make informed decisions regarding my care. Bring me wise and gentle caregivers who believe in my own dignity and the right to live until I die. Amen.

QUESTIONS TO PONDER

What are my options in care? Am I where I need to be right now for optimum comfort and quality of life?

TODAY I WILL

Not be afraid to talk with a family member or caregiver about whether hospice is an option for me.

SPIRIT

FOR THE SOUL THERE IS NEVER BIRTH OR DEATH. NOR,

HAVING ONCE BEEN, DOES IT EVER CEASE TO BE. IT IS

UNBORN, ETERNAL, EVER-EXISTING, UNDYING, AND

PRIMEVAL. IT IS NOT SLAIN WHEN THE BODY IS SLAIN.

—SACRED HINDU TEXT

My mother, Shirley, struggled with the fact that she would have roommates in the final weeks of her life. She wanted to come home where she could have a more dignified space of peace and privacy in which to die. But that wasn't possible, and a private room on the busy oncology floor was simply not available. Resolved, she squared her narrow shoulders and decided to "put up with" the strangers who, unlike her, would eventually leave the hospital under their own volition.

Anne, the most loving and caring of the roommates, the one with the most mendable body and a suitcase of humor, could make Shirley not only smile, but laugh out loud. One evening, after going through an exhausting day of medical procedures and visitors, Shirley looked forward to her bed and rest. But an hour later the two roommates were imbibing juice cocktails and betting on the upcoming Suns Basketball game, to which they both fully intended to listen. Their good spirits pervaded the room.

Because of Anne, Shirley learned to laugh again, to enjoy some of life's everyday offerings. In turn, Anne—an intermittent hospital patient—acknowledged that the friendship she'd developed with her dying roommate was the most meaningful hospital relationship she'd ever had.

Martha, Shirley's last roommate, an older woman with

impaired hearing, was prone to talking too loud and falling asleep to the abrasive noise of her television. At this point, Shirley was unable to get up without assistance, and food no longer held the remotest appeal. Despite her weakened condition and Martha's noisiness, the roommates soon grew to care about each other, calling for a nurse when the other needed one or talking together in the late night hours. When Martha's son walked in on them one particular morning, Shirley's eyes flashed open with such determination and unconcealed anger that he was taken aback. She told him of the early-morning interview Martha had endured with a brusque and hurried psychologist. "He was not in the least respectful of her," Shirley said, bristling. "He questioned her as if she had no brains left at all." Her brow furrowing, Shirley added in an exhausted whisper, "When Martha got mad and said she wasn't going to answer any more of his pompous questions, the man said she was acting childish. His tone was so patronizing. John, your mother did not deserve that kind of treatment."

Because of Shirley's advocacy, John decided that his mother's mental evaluation should not depend on just one doctor's analysis, that she deserved more. He was relieved, hopeful, empowered, and entirely open to taking a dying woman's witness as a voice close to God's. Shirley, in turn, saw that she could still make a difference in someone's life.

Despite her deteriorated physical condition, Shirley's spirit was very much alive and kicking in her final weeks. Her laughter and willful betting, her strong anger and defense of someone other than herself seemed remarkable. And yet, why should the idea of our spirits being stronger than our bodies surprise us? Story after story has been told of victims rallying or outliving predictions—usually due to their indomitable spirits.

In the business of dying, we can still be about the business of living. There are still times for rejoicing or feeling peace, for grieving or feeling worry, for hating or feeling indignation, for loving or feeling compassion.

PRAYER

O Great Spirit, on bad days—even on good days—it's exhausting to keep myself together, maintaining a minimum of interest or hope in the day. Help me to do what I can. Uplift my spirit with yours at the exact moment when I need it most and when others expect it least. Remind me that your great spirit dwells in mine forever. Amen.

QUESTION TO PONDER

Have I considered the idea that my spirit has the capability not only to uplift, but to outlive my body?

TODAY I WILL

Engage in one other person's life.

PRIORITIES

FOR EVERYTHING THERE IS A SEASON,

AND A TIME FOR EVERY MATTER UNDER HEAVEN. A

TIME TO BE BORN, AND A TIME TO DIE;

A TIME TO PLANT, AND A TIME TO PLUCK UP

    WHAT IS PLANTED;

A TIME TO KILL, AND A TIME TO HEAL;

A TIME TO BREAK DOWN,

AND A TIME TO BUILD UP;

A TIME TO WEEP, AND A TIME TO LAUGH;

A TIME TO MOURN, AND A TIME TO DANCE;

A TIME TO THROW AWAY STONES,

AND A TIME TO GATHER STONES TOGETHER;

A TIME TO EMBRACE,

AND A TIME TO REFRAIN FROM EMBRACING . . .

—ECCLESIASTES 3:1-5 (NRSV)

It is a question we often hear: if you knew this was the last day of your life, what would you do differently? What are the priorities you would choose? What choices would become most important to you? When we are not ill and not focused on our own impending death, we may be less particular about what is important. In everyday life, the small stuff can often become big stuff, and it may take the awareness of our own death to bring us to our senses. Suddenly, life takes on new meaning. Dying has an amazing ability to clarify our priorities.

Twenty years ago, Judy's son died of leukemia. He was only seventeen. The lessons he taught her about the value of priorities at the end of life remain fresh in her mind today. Judy said, "I can't tell you how important it was for me to protect my son's right to 'call the shots' as he neared the end of his life. He was dying at our home and I was like a mother wolf, guarding her pup. He became very particular about who he wanted visiting him and believe me, no one got in unless he OK'd it. He directed his personal priorities, and we respected them. It was so important to let him take charge of the time he had remaining."

Judy's son was adamant about who he wanted for visitors. You may need to be assertive in stating your own end-of-life priorities without apologies or explanations. Advocates, like Judy was for her son, can help you enforce those decisions. Sometimes the situations are awkward and uncomfortable. People may sense your need for control but not understand it. Gather your allies and embrace those who are most important to you. Time is precious; make no apologies for stating your wishes.

It was Christmas Eve and Jack knew he hadn't long to live. He had gathered his precious wife, married children, and grandchildren around him to celebrate what he knew would be their last holiday together. He had lived his life as a rancher and farmer. He had been strong and independent; he had been his family's primary provider. He knew the gathering this night was especially important; one last harvest of rich memories and love. A knock on the door, just before dinner was served, sent Jack's wife, Annie, scurrying first to the front door, and then back to her husband. "It's Angus, Jack. Shall I tell him it's a bad time to visit?" Annie had become his advocate; his gatekeeper of priorities throughout his illness. Jack's tired eyes reflected the candlelight from the dining-room table. His two-year-old grandson sat on the floor next to him, playing with a green tractor and plow. Jack spoke quietly, "He can come in."

Angus was tall, younger than Jack by twenty years, and quiet in his manner. He entered this sacred circle of family, almost with reverence, as if he understood the honor to visit at such a late and significant hour. He wore Western boots and a long, wool camel-colored coat, and he held his black felt cowboy hat awkwardly in front of him. No one spoke. Angus stood before Jack and looked at him. Jack returned his look with a level gaze. There was Christmas music playing softly on the radio. The timer on the oven buzzed, indicating the turkey was done. Still, no one in the room spoke. Jack and Angus had a complicated history together that both recalled but chose not to speak of. It hadn't always been friendly between them. But now, Angus's eyes reflected only respect and a disbelief that a man he had always seen as invincible was dying. Jack said nothing, nodded at Angus, leaned back in his chair and closed his eyes. Angus sighed, looked around the room at Annie and the children, and then quietly left. It was a time of embracing, orchestrated by Jack. He had opened his circle of priorities generously to allow one last person to step into it to say good-bye. When Angus left, Jack's ever-narrowing circle of priorities closed more tightly than ever around him.

The dying often begin to narrow the circle around themselves as death approaches. These circles become less and less wide, until at last it may be only you at the very center of your own life-circle. When once you appreciated neighbors and co-workers visiting, perhaps now you prefer only close friends and family. Consider it an act of love to draw that circle closer to yourself as you need to. No one knows your priorities better than you. Embrace or refrain from embracing. To everything there is a season, and a time for every purpose under heaven. It is your own sense of purpose that defines those end-of-life priorities. Embrace them and know your own time of peace.

PRAYER

Creator of purpose, I thank you for the gift of priorities in my life. Help me to discern what is most important as I face my own death. Grant me the control I need now to embrace only those who bring me peace. Amen.

QUESTIONS TO PONDER

Who shall enter into my innermost circle of embraces? Is there someone or something that I need now to refrain from embracing?

TODAY I WILL

Give myself permission to take control of my end-of-life priorities.

MEMORIES

YET I WILL NOT FORGET YOU . . . SEE! I HAVE INSCRIBED

YOU ON THE PALMS OF MY HANDS.

—ISAIAH 49:15-16 (NRSV)

We all want to know that our lives counted, and that we will be missed and remembered by our family and friends. In the children's grief group I (Sharon) facilitate, there is one activity that is a favorite. It brings even the shyest, withdrawn child into our circle of sharing. As homework for the following session, we ask the children to bring an item that reminds them of the person who died. No matter their age or level of acceptance, you can see the light in their eyes as they whisper to one another: "I'll bring Mama's picture" or "Grandpa gave me his watch." It is the beginning of a lesson for these grieving children that memories and love remain, and sharing stories can help heal their broken hearts.

One week, we were comfortably seated, cookies and juice balanced on napkin-covered laps. The storytelling began. "Who would like to share the item they brought?" I asked. Seven-year-old Sarah shared her parent's wedding picture. Twelve-year-old Josh proudly told the story of his father's swimming awards as the group passed around a worn shoe box filled with medals strung on red, white, and blue ribbons.

Ten-year-old Michael sat, hands in pockets, carefully studying the floor. "Michael, did you bring an item to share?" I asked gently. It's OK for the children to pass, but Michael smiled coyly and shrugged his shoulders. "Well, I didn't bring anything to show, but my grandpa did teach me to wiggle my ears!" To the delight of all of us in the circle, Michael magically wiggled his ears, slowly and in unison. The group members laughed and applauded. Suddenly, Grandpa and his memory were alive and notably carved, not only in his grandson Michael's stories and radiant smile, but in the imagination and heart of each of us.

Rickie Lee Jones has been quoted as saying, "You never know when you're creating a memory." Whatever stage of life we're in, it's a good thing to acknowledge that we will be remembered and loved by our friends and family for those defining moments that created a memory.

PRAYER

Lord, keep me alive always in my loved ones' memories. Help me today to continue to create moments that last and to remember that sometimes it is the smallest event that bears the most lasting mark. Amen.

QUESTION TO PONDER

How do I want to be remembered?

TODAY I WILL

Create one lasting memory with a loved one.

ℒℰ𝒢𝒜𝒞𝒴

MEMORY CAN TELL US ONLY WHAT WE WERE, IN COM-
PANY WITH THOSE WE LOVED; IT CANNOT HELP US
FIND WHAT EACH OF US, ALONE, MUST NOW BECOME.
YET NO PERSON IS REALLY ALONE; THOSE WHO LIVE
NO MORE ECHO STILL WITHIN OUR THOUGHTS AND
WORDS, AND WHAT THEY DID HAS BECOME WOVEN
INTO WHO WE ARE.

—JEWISH PRAYER

Memory is a valuable tool, for it takes us out of our small rooms and back into the memorable places and times of our lives. It was Ralph Waldo Emerson who said death puts lives into perspective. And so it is that we can look back on our lives—whether they were short or long, whether we had children or not, whether they were complex and noteworthy or full of abundant simplicity— and think about both sides of our legacy: that which we've been given and that which we're leaving behind.

Ludmilla's son Tom had debated a long time about the gift he was bringing, worrying that it would cause his mother not happiness but grief about all that she'd be missing out on in the years ahead. He gazed at the enlarged photograph of seven children and twelve grandchildren in one somewhat perfect collective pose. Little Matthew, clutched in his brother's arms, looked, as usual, as though he was protesting even the momentary loss of freedom. Tall John had his arm draped around his sister Lisa's shoulders, her face looking suspiciously stricken, as though her breath were being squeezed out of her. Tom's own face and those of several of his siblings beamed mischievously at the photographer. Photograph in hand, Tom entered his mother's room.

Ludmilla seemed lost in the hospital bed, a frail, pale miniature of the vital woman she'd been only months before. "Mom, I brought you something I hope you'll enjoy." He placed the gift in her hands.

She leaned over to study the photograph. She smiled, scanning the picture from one end to the other. Tom could see her eyes focusing on each face, her expression never changing. Then she leaned back in her bed, closed her eyes, and hugged the photograph to her chest. "Thank you, Tom." In the days ahead she looked at the photograph often, always with a smile on her face.

The picture was a representation of Ludmilla's legacy: large, diverse, full of vitality, ongoing. Ludmilla could let go of her life as she knew it, but it would continue in the lives of her children and grandchildren. She could gaze at the picture and into the faces of her offspring and know that she had done good work, and that because of her influence, these people would be making their marks on the world. She hoped that each would leave a positive contribution. The odds were favorable that most of them would.

Perhaps Ludmilla thought about the other end of the spectrum, too. The one in which *she* was the receiver of *her* parents' and grandparents' legacies: those of her grandmother who'd left the old country for a harrowing trip across the sea . . . those of her mother's fight and survival during the flu epidemic . . . those of her own lessons during the Depression. Ultimately Ludmilla's children and grandchildren were the result of a greater team effort.

Legacies can come in much smaller packages, too. Take Marian. She's a spry eighty-year-old woman who still vividly remembers a childhood incident. One day, after yet another one of her tantrums, her mother had turned in exasperation to Marian's grandmother and said, "I don't know what we're going to do about Marian." Today, seven and a half decades later, Marian still remembers her grandmother's exact words: "She'll be all right. I wouldn't give two cents for a kid without spunk." Marian said that single comment came back to her again and again through the years, giving her courage and determination when she needed them most. I doubt that Marian's grandmother had any idea of the magnitude of her small but lasting legacy.

PRAYER

When I can't sleep and when I worry about my state of affairs, help me to remember who was woven into my life, making a difference. Help me discern where I may have made a difference. Though my memory be short and my understanding limited, remind me that even the smallest piece is just the tip of the legacy I'm leaving behind. Amen.

QUESTION TO PONDER

What have I said or done that may be part of my legacy?

TODAY I WILL

Recall one person's words or actions that were woven into who I became.

UNFINISHED BUSINESS

WHEN LIFE IS CUT SHORT, WE CAN REACH OUT TO
HELP THOSE FACING DEATH. WE CAN PROVIDE THE
TOOLS TO SAY GOOD-BYE TO THIS WORLD AND HELLO
TO THE NEXT.

—THE MOM'S DEVOTIONAL BIBLE (NIV)

Betsy was moving to a new community. She lay awake at night and made mental lists, deciding where her mother's antique china hutch would fit best in her next home and worried about whether the storage space in her new garage was adequate. During the day, Betsy called her friends and arranged breakfast and lunch dates as a way of saying good-bye. She mailed change-of-address cards, called the newspaper, the utility company, the garbage collector. She was leaving town, and the list of things she needed to do before she left seemed endless.

How trivial this example of transition seems when we compare it to the thought of facing our own or a loved one's dying. Thinking of the unfinished tasks that face us at that most difficult time in our lives can be overwhelming. Where does one begin with the calls, the lists, and the saying good-bye, or, better, how does one begin?

Unfinished business has many faces. Jack, always the banker, tended to the practical matters, such as double-checking financial affairs and wills, making sure insurance and trust documents were properly signed and administered. It was helpful to him to have someone he trusted, like his wife and attorney friend, help him with these details. A young mother accomplished some of her unfinished business with a video camera and her husband's help. She wrote out her hopes and dreams for her young children's futures. Then, tearfully but bravely, she recorded her thoughts for them to watch when they were older and could better understand. Reminiscing or reviewing our lives with photo albums is another way to conduct our unfinished business with our loved ones. It facilitates storytelling, and plants our memory deep in our loved ones' hearts. Letter writing, too, can meet our need for closure with our loved ones. Although it can be painful to actually say good-bye, it offers the opportunity for expressing our feelings, such as I love you, thank you, and good-bye.

Sometimes, we need to say a special good-bye. Tom loved his cattle. Every day, he had tended and nurtured his herd. Some he had named, and only he could tell the difference between one red-and-white cow and another. Just days before his death, he asked his sons to take him for a drive to see the cows. Helping their ill father into the car, they carefully propped him with pillows. It was just a short drive to the pasture and back. But it was joy-filled unfinished business for Tom to see his cows one last time and to be able to say good-bye. And his sons treasure the memory of that final gift they gave their father, helping him complete his unfinished business.

Perhaps it's doing something you've always wanted to do. My friend Kay took dancing lessons. Jackie had her first hot air balloon ride. Sometimes our unfinished business cannot be planned, but unexpected events may bring us the blessing of completeness. A photo in *The Dunn County Herald* showed the first baby born in the new year. The baby's grandfather, who had been ill for a long time, died that same day. Beneath the baby's first photograph was this statement: "Baylee was born two hours and 45 minutes before her grandpa Dave died. He got to see her and hold her." What better unfinished business can there be than that?

There is a national organization called the Dream Foundation, which grants wishes for terminally ill adults. (There's also one for children called the Make A Wish Foundation.) The Dream Foundation's brochure states their goal is to help the "final days of terminally ill adults be filled with peace and completion." And they accomplish that regularly by arranging family reunions, helping with travel plans to a fun destination, or connecting the person dying with a lifelong dream. They are in the business of unfinished business, helping the dying let go and move toward a sense of peace and completion.

What unfinished business do you have? Is there a relationship to mend or someone you need to thank? Are there practical matters that you need taken care of before you can rest? Your dying wish may be to complete some unfinished business that only you can name. With the support of loved ones, name those wishes and then get on with the important task of completing them. Mark them off your own mental checklist and feel the sense of peace it brings.

PRAYER

Lord, I have much unfinished business to do. Help me prioritize which matters are most pressing. Bring me loved ones to help in saying good-bye to this world before saying hello to the next. Amen.

QUESTION TO PONDER

What are the most pressing matters on my "unfinished business" list?

TODAY I WILL

Complete one item on my list: tell someone I appreciate them, write a letter, or make a phone call to say good-bye with love.

GATHERINGS

HERE BEGINS THE OPEN SEA. HERE BEGINS THE GLORI-
OUS ADVENTURE, THE ONLY ONE ABREAST WITH
HUMAN CURIOSITY, THE ONLY ONE THAT SOARS AS
HIGH AS ITS HIGHEST LONGING. LET US ACCUSTOM
OURSELVES TO REGARD DEATH AS A FORM OF LIFE
WHICH WE DO NOT YET UNDERSTAND; LET US LEARN
TO LOOK UPON IT WITH THE SAME EYE THAT LOOKS
UPON BIRTH; AND SOON OUR MIND WILL BE ACCOM-
PANIED TO THE STEPS OF THE TOMB WITH THE SAME
GLAD EXPECTATION AS GREETS A BIRTH.

—MAURICE MAETERLINCK

The Native people in the Alaskan villages intentionally keep death and dying a natural part of life. They willingly take an active role in the ending of their earthly lives, seeming to know intuitively when meaningful life is drawing to a close. Few require the services of a doctor to tell them they are terminal; instead they enter the final phase easily and naturally. One who was especially involved in the planning of her final days was a woman by the name of Old Sarah.

Father Murray Trelease, a parish priest who served the Alaskan Indian villages during the 1960s, recorded the events surrounding her death. He received a message from Old Sarah summoning him to her village. He gathered four members of her family and flew them to Arctic Village on the designated day. By the time he arrived, there was quite a gathering of people for this undisputed matriarch of both the family and the community. Father Murray reported that "the next day she prayed for all the members of her family. At noon we had a great celebration of the Eucharist in her cabin, complete with all the hymns and prayers. Old Sarah loved every minute of it, joined in the prayers and the singing and was quite bright throughout the service. Then we all left and, at six in the evening, she died."

Father Murray said that for the next two days the entire village turned out to prepare Sarah's body, clean her cabin, make a coffin, dig the grave in the frozen ground, and cook vast quantities of food—much of which Sarah had bought for the occasion.

The entire village packed into the church for the funeral, accompanied the coffin to the graveyard, and joined in the great feast that followed.

Too often those in Sarah's slippers are simply asked "Are you comfortable?" when what they really want to be asked is "What can I do for you?" If asked that question, the response might be so clear, creative, and determined that it would take everyone's breath away. Personally, I'd like to surprise those around me by doing more than simply lying there thinking about my comfort level. I'd like to hand over an invitation list and a grocery list in order to throw a party with good food, music, laughter, meaningful conversation . . . with my recliner right in the middle of it all. I want to be like the man who attended a friend's funeral, heard all the nice things that were said about his friend, and decided that he'd rather hear those things while he was still alive. So he did. He invited his family and friends in for a living funeral. I want to be like Joyce who told her husband—when he delicately asked if she liked a certain hymn—"Listen! This is my funeral, I'll pick out the hymns." I want to be like Dennis who told his friends to wear jeans and sweatshirts to his funeral because the reception would be at Lake Maria State Park, one of the places he loved. And, he said, *he* would be wearing jeans and a sweatshirt.

But most of all, I want to be like Sarah, who called the

shots to the very last minute, who took the time to bless those she cared about, who intuitively knew when she was going to die and arranged all the hoopla around her demise. Stories prevail of dying people who seemed more or less in charge of their own deaths. They didn't go until they'd seen the one person or the one event that they were waiting to see. Only then, did they willingly—even willfully—die.

What would happen if we planned our own gathering, in whatever form that might take? Besides our own gratification of being host to a memorable and sacred assemblage, our guests might also be left with something extra to think about, like how wonderful it is to participate more fully—not just at the beginning and middle of life—but at the end of life.

PRAYER

Dear God, I want to leave my isolation and offer human warmth. I want to enfold others, providing a time and space to give gifts of love and ritual and to receive theirs as well. Give me voice to speak and energy to move into a gathering that offers memories, blessings, and solidity for me and for others. Amen.

QUESTION TO PONDER

What kind of gathering—small or large—would I plan before my dying hour?

TODAY I WILL

Think of one or more persons I would like to invite to my room.

HEALING

EVERYONE CAN HEAL, YOU KNOW. A SMILE CAN HEAL,
A LISTENING EAR, A GENTLE TOUCH. . . . ALL THOSE
THINGS. WE FORGET THAT HEALERS AREN'T OTHER
PEOPLE; THEY'RE US.

—ANONYMOUS

Elizabeth's fingers were busy with the fringes of her afghan. Thomas, her husband of fifty years, sat next to her bed and watched her quietly. He had always been there for her, in sickness and in health, as they had vowed to one another so many years before. He had protected her and provided for her. She, in turn, had loved him and cared for him. It was hard for him now. He had watched her gradual decline in health over the past several years, as the effects of Alzheimer's disease claimed not only her mind, but her body as well. So many times after he'd left her room at the local nursing home, he had prayed for a cure or, at least, a reprieve from the slide he watched her caught in: slipping every day, further and further from the person he once knew and still loved. Today, as always, even with God's help, he felt powerless to help her.

But today was different for Elizabeth, because she was actively dying. In the past, Thomas might've seen glimpses of his former wife. He'd be standing in her room and, unexpectedly, her gaze would fall on him in bright recognition and she would ask, "Thomas, where are the children?" or "Tom, bring me my brown handbag." Then, just as suddenly, she would be gone, lost in her own ramblings and thoughts that he felt no part of. But today, since breakfast, when he'd arrived for his daily visit, he'd seen no flicker of recognition from Elizabeth. She lay quietly on her bed, covered by the colorful afghan she'd knit herself, her eyes closed and only her fingers moving. The nurses told him she was in a light coma. "Just be with her," they advised. He wondered what good it could do.

Several times throughout that long day, Thomas looked at his watch and thought about leaving. It was hard to sit and watch his wife so unresponsive. He tried talking to her, telling her he loved her. He ran his fingers down the side of her face, feeling the familiar wrinkles and softness of her skin. The nurses came in to turn, rub, and reposition her. There was no response from Elizabeth. Thomas himself felt sick as the day wore on; from fear and sadness because he was losing his wife, but also from his own inability to save her from a disease he didn't understand. All day he sat with her, as their children, the nurses, doctors, and minister came and went.

Toward evening, they were again alone. Elizabeth's breathing changed, becoming less regular and with longer intervals of quiet between each breath. Thomas knelt by her bed and took her restless hands in his. "Elizabeth, I love you," he whispered. What happened next, Thomas would later tell his children, was a direct answer to his prayer for their mother's healing. Suddenly, Elizabeth opened her bright hazel eyes, gazed straight into Thomas's own with the loving recognition of a wife for her husband, and said clearly, "The door is open!" It was an image of faith they had both believed in and talked about long before Elizabeth had become ill: the vision of a door opening to heaven, a door that they believed led from this world to the next, to life eternal. Two deep breaths followed, and then she was gone. Thomas laid his head on her still hands and wept.

Thomas talked of the healing that had taken place. "Your mother did that for my sake, you know?" he said with tears in his eyes. "She knew I was sick with sorrow and that I wanted her to be at peace. Imagine the resolve it took on her part to come back one last time to give me that glimpse of recognition! To speak to me of the open door! It was such a comfort to me!"

And what of Elizabeth's healing? We should always understand that the sense of hearing and presence is intact until the very last moment of death. Thomas's gentle touches, his loving words, his presence at her bedside were healing to her. She died in the arms of love as she glimpsed her own open door. What greater sense of peace and healing can one experience than that?

PRAYER

O great Physician, empower me as a healer. Surround me, too, with those who aren't afraid to smile at me, hold me, and listen to me. Perhaps with our ministering to one another, the miraculous healing of spirit will touch us all. Amen.

QUESTION TO PONDER

Who was my healer today? This week? This month?

TODAY I WILL

Become a healer myself with a smile, a touch, a word.

HOPE

I forgot to take the wind chimes in from my garden last fall. As I high-stepped through the snow drifts in the frigid cold of January to fill the bird feeders, the chimes jangling next to me sounded crisp, sharp, impatient for winter to end. I, too, longed for summer. Because winter is not my favorite season, I imagined my garden in July; nodding larkspur and tall Russian sage, fragrant marigolds and velvety hydrangeas unfurling on crowded branches. My hope for summer and light and heat sustained me. I knew with certainty that seasons would change and summer would come. This is hope: the positive expectation of things to come. The simple wind chimes, their shadows swaying in the weak winter sun, reminded me. And I was sustained through the darkest days of winter.

Hope is powerful medicine, one that can enrich and even sustain our lives. Hope can help us continue living despite uncertainty. Hope is a choice we make even in the face of darkest reality. With the green branches of hope in our hearts, the singing bird of coping, acceptance, and peace may come.

But hope is ever-changing. Deb was a young woman of thirty, diagnosed with a rare form of breast cancer. In the beginning of her battle with this fierce opponent, she hoped for a cure. She researched her disease and sought out the best care and doctors medicine could offer. She drew on her own inner resources of intelligence and good access to information. It gave her hope and made her stress more tolerable. When her doctors informed her the prognosis was poor, Deb did not lose hope, because she knew hopelessness was helplessness. Instead, she hoped for compassionate care from her doctors and looked forward to a future that she would fill with passionate living, day by day. She tried to remain optimistic, determined, and positive—all key elements in coping that she knew might help extend her life. She joined a support group and found doctors and nurses who took time to listen. Deb was discovering hope in the face of her own reality: that she harbored a disease that would eventually take her life.

As her hope changed and her disease progressed even further, Deb created new goals for herself. One was to write a book about her experiences. She took writing courses and met new friends. Another was to spend quality time with her husband and young son. And yet another was to create a perennial flower garden in her backyard. Her green branches brought many singing birds in those months of hoping. She wasn't denying her situation, but rather working at maintaining hope. Deb was a survivor.

When complications set in and Deb became gravely ill again, her hope changed. She hoped for friends and family to remain close, for freedom from pain and good symptom control. She still made plans for her future, but they were more short-term and specific.

She lived each day with a sense of humor, a fierceness to avoid despair, and a realistic hope that enhanced her quality of life.

Research studies reinforce the benefits of maintaining hope in the face of serious illness. Positive feelings can boost the immune system, enhance patient outcomes, and may even effect the course of disease. The danger of this thinking is in stating that a positive state of mind can cure disease because it may place the blame on the patient if and when a disease progresses, in spite of hope and optimism. Hope is not a cure-all; rather, it's an important component of good coping. Hope, that green branch in our hearts, may bring the singing birds of acceptance and peace. St. Augustine said, "O Lord, our God, under the shadow of Thy wings, let us hope." So, too, may you find sustaining power and comfort in the loving arms and shadows of caregivers and in your own inner strengths, which offer the singing bird and reassurances of hope.

PRAYER

God of gardens and light and shadows, help me to sustain green branches in the midst of depression, fear, and despair. Bring singing birds and peaceful understanding to my own situation. Allow me the power of hope as I draw on my inner resources, the loving care that surrounds me, and on you, Lord. Amen.

QUESTIONS TO PONDER

How can I work at maintaining hope? What resources can I draw on to help me sustain the green branches of hope in my heart?

TODAY I WILL

Name one thing I hope for today; name one person who can help give me hope with their reassuring presence and then ask them to help empower me with hopefulness.

BEYOND THIS LIFE

THIS WORLD IS NOT CONCLUSION;

A SEQUEL STANDS BEYOND,

INVISIBLE, AS MUSIC,

BUT POSITIVE, AS SOUND.

—EMILY DICKINSON

Bill, a slight and gentle man with thick, dark hair and a penchant for whistling Dixieland jazz, lived with his wife, Mo, in Kendal, in the northwest corner of England. Their bungalow looked out over the hills on one side and a tidy garden on the other side. Each morning, rain or shine, Bill pulled on his Wellington knee boots and putzed among the flower beds and rose bushes. When he discovered he was sick, it was too late to save him. He died on a cool spring morning.

Mo felt all those things that everyone in grief feels when they lose a loved one. Sometimes she ranted and raged. She stomped around the house yelling, "Why did you leave me? We had so much more we wanted to do together!" She tried to cope by putting his things out of sight: his Wellies in the depths of the hall closet, his brush and toiletries in the back of the bathroom cabinet. Just days after Bill's funeral, she was startled to discover his mud-spattered green Wellies on the doormat beside the back door—as if he'd just come in from working in the garden. She eyed them all day, waiting, then finally raged, "Bill, you bloody fool, why can't you just talk to me?" The next morning, she found his hairbrush on the lip of the sink where Bill always left it. In the days that followed, Mo would catch his scent, a strong nutty smell that was as familiar as his boots and his silver-backed hairbrush. Once she even heard a few bars of "Sweet Georgia Brown" whistled sweet and low in the kitchen.

Years have passed since Bill's death, and Mo now wonders which of these incidents really occurred. At the time, they were as real as Bill himself had been. She never once felt as if she were going crazy, nor did she ever feel fear. "Those small evidences of Bill being nearby were simply comforting, and they helped me get through that first horrible year."

Barbara, from the deserts of Arizona, tells another kind of story, one about an unusual dream she had. In this dream, her mother appears, although she'd died many years before. Barbara said she remembers saying to her, almost angrily, "I've been searching for you for a long time. Where have you been?" Her mother responds, "Why I've been busy, very busy, and happy, too." Barbara asks her more questions. She discovers that her mother is in charge of children, children who have died young and are in need of supervision. Barbara awoke feeling a deep happiness. She said her mother would be "a perfectly wonderful caregiver for God's youngest children. I love thinking about her in that way. The dream gave me so much comfort about her premature death."

Poems, books, movies, and stories abound with haunting, poignant, or ethereal glimpses of life after death. Almost all cultures, and certainly most of the world's great religions, maintain a belief in life after death. Descriptions of what that life might look like vary; the recordings are as illuminating as they are mind-boggling.

Authors Rodegast and Stanton in *Emmanuel's Book* maintain that "You do not cease to exist at death. You go through the doorway of death alive and there is no altering of the consciousness. It is not a strange land you go to but a land of living reality where the growth process is a continuation . . . Death is only a passage through, a time release."

PRAYER

Father, Mother, Spirit, give me peace about dying. I want to feel—really feel deep down in my bones—that my spirit will go on, that there's more to life than the one I'm now living. Grant me a glimpse that this world is not conclusion, a glimpse that will sustain me and feel as positive as sound. Amen.

QUESTION TO PONDER

What would I imagine the next world to look like? Who will I see? What will I be doing?

TODAY I WILL

Try to remember a time when I, or someone I know, glimpsed another world.

$\mathcal{L}ETTING\ GO$

One of the greatest concerns during both our living and our dying is being separated from our loved ones and how these loved ones will care for themselves without us. Death is sometimes seen as a failure, as a cop-out before the job is done. A mother can feel terrible distress about a handicapped son's ability to live effectively and efficiently after she's gone. A husband worries about his wife's ability to care for their children without his partnership. A child feels anxious about leaving her parents when they can't seem to stop crying. A spouse or partner frets about his partner's ability to get along without him.

Nathaniel, a respected school superintendent most of his working years, struggled with congestive heart failure during the last months of his life. He seemed to bounce back and forth between mental alertness and a fuzzy muddle. One day, he opened his eyes, saw his wife Norma walking by, and yelled, "Get a Buick! You must sell the car and get a Buick!" His wild shouting took Norma aback. She sorrowfully decided that he was "out of it" that day, especially because their car wasn't that old. But his daughter Leona saw something different. Her father's TV was often on, along with an advertising campaign for Buick's latest model. Several ads had the same image: a Buick is traveling down a treacherous road through harsh weather, complete with branches falling, lightning flashing, thunder bellowing. The ride inside the Buick, however, is quiet, secure, and serene. That's what Leona decided her father wanted for her mother after he left: a life that was calm, without problems and anxieties.

Another man, Kenny, a small-town hardware store owner, waited until he had a brain tumor with only a limited time to speak before he suddenly started worrying. He was terribly concerned that his wife wasn't prepared to live without him. She had no driver's license and had never done any of the family bookkeeping, and Kenny had never consulted her about major decisions. How would she be able to deal with the complex issues he hadn't prepared her for? He drifted in and out of a coma, repeatedly mumbling about these anxieties.

What would it be like if we stopped worrying? What if we let the worries go? Is it possible to stop stewing about the things over which we no longer have control? What if we were told that the problems that torment us would be worked out in the best possible way, even if that way proved different or unfamiliar to us? What if we were assured that the people we love would experience what they need to experience in order to become who they're intended to become? A printed sign hanging on the wall of a Minneapolis hospital corridor says: "Good morning. Today I will be handling all of your problems. Please remember that I do not need your help. God."

We must remind ourselves that the loved ones we leave behind may struggle for a while, but they'll be fine. They'll figure it out. And they'll be stronger people for the struggle. Nathaniel would be interested to know that a year after he died, his wife Norma had a minor car accident with their car. She decided to trade it in—for a Buick. Her life seems to be moving peacefully along with few critical problems. Kenny would be happy to know that his wife learned how to drive a car, is managing their finances with only a few setbacks, and has handled complex decisions on her own.

Worrying about the future of our loved ones is no reason to hang on, especially when it means drifting in and out of a coma, hovering anxiously at the edge of life. The bottom line is to do what we can *when* we can, but also to recognize the other times when we must simply let go.

PRAYER

God, help me stop worrying about those things over which I have no control. Help me remember that you—with your much larger perspective and your much higher wisdom—will take over where I'm leaving off. I will stop fretting about the primroses, the finances, and the lives of my loved ones. They're in good hands. Amen.

QUESTION TO PONDER

What am I restless about?

TODAY I WILL

Let go of my worries.

GOING HOME

WHY WOULD IT BE SUPPOSED THAT ONE'S CREATIVE
ABILITY CEASES AT THE MOMENT CONSCIOUSNESS
LEAVES THE PHYSICAL? THE INSTANT THAT THE SELF
RELEASES FROM THE BODY THERE IS LIGHT, THERE IS
PEACE, THERE IS FREEDOM, THERE IS HOME.

—PAT RODEGAST AND JUDITH STANTON

A story that delighted my mother, Shirley, during her last week was one told by Ted Menten in his book *Gentle Closings*. He asked a group of children what they thought was going to happen when they died. Heaven was a popular destination:

"How will you get there?" he asked.
"An angel will come get me," replied Wendy.
"Beamed up like on 'Star Trek,'" said Bobby.
"I want Lassie to take me," said little Sharon.
"But Lassie's only a dog!" said a disapproving Bobby.
"I know, but Lassie always knows how to get home."

My mother missed her beloved cocker spaniel, Missy, and she approved of little Sharon's point. But the business of "going home" was what was really on her mind. For one thing, she looked forward to talking to my dad about decisions and worries she'd faced in the years since his death. For another, she was looking forward to getting out of bed, permanently. She was also interested in and curious about the next journey.

My mother had no illusions about the short time

remaining for her. That openness may be why she and Ruth, her oncology nurse, had such a positive relationship. Ruth was a tall, competent, almond-skinned woman, blessed with a calmness of spirit, who knew all about life and death and its many messy details. She ministered to my mother's needs from a deep wellspring of efficiency, gentleness, and reverence.

"Shirley," she said one day after a series of my mother's questions, "I admire the way you stay in charge of your life."

"Ruth," my mother said one evening, "I feel calmer and more collected on the days you're working."

It seemed no coincidence that my mother's last day on earth coincided with Ruth's last day before her vacation. Gently Ruth turned my mother's frail body, efficiently changing the bedding at the same time. When she finished, she simply gazed at my mother. Then she leaned across the bed and kissed her cheek. "Shirley, I've enjoyed our friendship." Unresponsive most of the day, but always one to reach out and touch another, my mother curved her hand around Ruth's arm and squeezed ever so gently.

Ruth turned to the window, where the evening shadows were gathering. She smiled and spoke, again. "Shirley, let's leave the light on. Those angels, they love the light, and they're close by tonight. When you're ready, they'll come right through this window and gather you up." My mother's face had been impassive, almost vacant for many hours, but now it broke into a small, but genuine, smile. Ruth nodded and walked out.

The peacefulness that remained in that cubicle was as close to holiness as I ever expect to feel again on this earth. The signs were there; the time was close at hand. In the silence, broken only by my mother's oddly pronounced breathing, I remember—as though in a trance—putting my arm around her shoulders, and whispering my thankfulness for her life. "Go to those angels, Mom. Find Dad. And Grandpa and Grandma and all those who wait for you." Not wanting to let go of her, I repeated her favorite 23rd Psalm. By the time we'd "walked through the valley of the shadow of death" her breathing had stopped.

And suddenly the room was empty . . . as if a gathering had left . . . as if my mother needed to get on with the rest of her life. The body that remained was barely recognizable, so empty of spirit I was taken aback. I was suddenly conscious of how real and large the spirit is, that when it leaves the body, it takes the body's very essence with it. I felt numbness and shock at the speed of this transference. I couldn't grieve that night. How could I? I knew without a doubt that angels or Dad and others—maybe even Missy— had arrived to lead my mother home.

Rabindranath Tagore may have said it best: "Death is not putting out the light. It is only extinguishing a lamp because the day has come." Going from home to Home may be like that. I think it was so for my mother.

PRAYER

Creator of Light and Love, drive away the shadows that linger around my bed. Overpower and empower this weak lamp of mine with the kind of light that brings peace, freedom, and home. Amen.

QUESTION TO PONDER

Whom would I wish to lead me Home?

TODAY I WILL

Light a candle and be reminded that its flame is only the tiniest representation of the light to come.

STORIES

MY NAME IS ELIZABETH. I AM A VESSEL FILLED WITH
STORIES. PLEASE ACCEPT MY STORIES AND TREASURE
THEM.

—DONNA O'TOOLE

Everyone loves a good story. Stories have the ability to connect us in our imaginations or in the reality of everyday living. Donna O'Toole, a lecturer and storyteller herself, tells us that when we trust one another enough to share our life experiences as stories, we validate and witness for one another. Stories serve to teach or inform us, to normalize a situation, to connect us with a bigger picture, and to honor our or someone else's memory.

Many stories within these pages are someone else's. Experiences have been shared that teach us valuable lessons about living and dying. Donna O'Toole said, "Grief is about connection . . . not separation," and indeed, all of these sacred stories connect us in their remembering. When we experience loss and grieve, it is good to be connected. Connectedness often brings comfort and understanding.

As this book of meditations evolved, many stories were told. Each person shared with the understanding that their story might be helpful to someone else. And in the telling, it made them a part of the process of healing connectedness.

Picture a roomful of compassionate listeners, and you sitting among them. Imagine you are invited to tell a story that holds great meaning for you. Perhaps it relates to your illness and how you've dealt with it through the past months or years. Or maybe it is an encounter you've experienced with someone else and the lessons it taught you. Can you trust enough to tell your own story? Imagine yourself being invited to the center of a circle of story-tellers and listeners. Rest quietly there, close your eyes, compose yourself, and begin. Your story will be accepted and treasured.

Although it happened over thirty years ago, Dee's experience still brings tears to her eyes. She shared her story in loving memory of her father. Dee said the lesson it teaches is about the permanence of the human spirit. Dee's father had been ill and in the hospital. When she had a dream about her father one night, she awoke puzzled by its meaning. In the dream, he had said to her, "I'm OK, Dee. Everything is all right." In the morning, she dismissed it, until her mother called to say her father had died during the night. Dee understood then that her father's spirit and love had transcended human understanding and his spirit had touched her with the powerful love and protectiveness of a father for his daughter. Dee's story connects us all as we relate to those feelings we ourselves may have experienced when someone we loved died.

So what is your story? Can you choose a trusted listener to share it with? You, too, are a vessel filled with stories that can heal both you and someone else in the telling. Empty your vessel into the arms of another and experience the comfort it can bring.

PRAYER

Lord, help me to tell my stories. Provide a loving, nonjudgmental listener to receive them. Help me to share with clarity of thought and to trust in the process. Allow the telling to connect and heal and honor us both. Amen.

QUESTIONS TO PONDER

Who is the trusted listener closest to me? Is there someone less obvious that would also benefit from my stories?

TODAY I WILL

Empty my vessel of at least one story that asks to be told, and trust that it will be treasured for its telling.

Bibliography

The authors gratefully acknowledge the following sources for their contributions to this book. Any omissions are unintentional and will be corrected upon future printings.

Remember Me
Hegi, Ursula. *Stones from the River*. New York: Simon & Schuster, 1994.

Lessons
Edwards, Deanna. *Grieving: The Pain and the Promise*. Salt Lake City: Covenant Communications, 1989; *A Healing Affair of the Heart*, sound cassette, copyright © 1974. Rock Canyon Music Publishers.
Hamblen, Stuart. *This Old House*. Hamblen Music, 1954. Used by permission.

Scars
Nouwen, Henri. "True Friends," *Guideposts* (January 1999).
Pitkin, Dorothy. "The Cold Literal Moments," *The Massachusetts Review, Inc.*, 1973.
Jeffrey, Shirley Holzer. "Louie," *Death: The Final Stage of Growth* by Elisabeth Kübler-Ross. Englewood Cliffs, N.J.: Prentice Hall, 1975.

Living Fully
Shaw, George Bernard. Lecture, "Art and Public Money," at Brighton, 1907. Copyright © 1977 the Trustees of the British Museum, Governors and Guardians of the National Gallery of Ireland, and the Royal Academy of Dramatic Art.

Character
Keleman, Stanley. *Living Your Dying*. Berkeley: Center Press, 1985.
Conner, Joan. "When Mountains Move," *Loss of the Ground Note: Women Writing About the Loss of their Mothers* by Helen Vozenilek. Los Angeles: Clothespin Fever Press, 1991.
Carmody, John Tully. *God Is No Illusion, Meditations on the End of Life*. Valley Forge, Pa.: Trinity Press International, 1997.

Final Wishes
Hammarskjöld, Dag. *Markings*. Boston: GK Hall, 1976.
Beisser, Arnold. "Life, Death and Dignity," *Los Angeles Times*. 8 April 1990, sec. E, pp. 1-2, 10.
Beisser, Arnold R. *A Graceful Passage*. New York: Doubleday, 1990.
Brody, Jane. "Patients Want Their Wishes Heard at Life's End," *St. Paul Pioneer Press*. 20 February 1999.

Fear
Marshall, Peter. *Refresh My Heart: A Daily Prayer Journal* by Paul C. Brownlow. Fort Worth, Tex.: Brownlow Publishing Company, 1991.
Epstein, Charlotte. *Nursing the Dying Patient: Learning Processes for Interaction*. Reston, Va.: Publishing Co., Inc, 1975.
Howlett, Debbie. "Payton Has Liver Disease: NFL great needs transplant." *USA Today*. 3 February 1999, Sports, sec. 1C.

Control
Lomask, Milton. *The Biographer's Craft*. New York: Harper & Row, 1986.
Albom, Mitch. *Tuesdays with Morrie: An Old Man, a Young Man, and Life's Greatest Lesson*. New York: Doubleday, 1997.

Loneliness
Goldberg, Natalie. *Wild Mind: Living the Writer's Life*. New York: Bantam Books, 1990.

Dying Alone
Kübler-Ross, Elisabeth. *The Wheel of Life: A Memoir of Living and Dying*. New York: Scribner, 1997.
Callanan, Maggie and Patricia Kelley. *Final Gifts: Understanding the Special Awareness, Needs, and Communications of the Dying*. N.Y.: Poseidon Press, 1992.

Dark Nights
Sondheim, Stephen, and James Lapine. *Into the Woods*. New York: Theatre Communications Group, 1989.

Permission by Music Theater Int'l.

Carmody, John Tully. *God Is No Illusion: Meditations on the End of Life.* Valley Forge, Pa.: Trinity Press International, 1997.

Dickinson, Emily. *#419. Final Harvest, Emily Dickinson's Poems.* Compiled by Thomas H. Johnson. Boston: Little, Brown & Co., 1961.

Karnes, Barbara. *Gone from My Sight: The Dying Experience.* Self-published, 1986.

Words

Karnes, Barbara. *Gone from My Sight: The Dying Experience.* Self-published, 1986.

Hochstadt, Adrienne Reiner. "Cancer Talk Is a Language That's Learned Only through Experience." Reprinted in the *Star Tribune* from *Journal of the American Medical Association* 280, no. 16 (October 28, 1998): 1385.

Angels

Palmer, Tobias. *An Angel in My House.* San Francisco: HarperSanFrancisco, 1995.

Browning, Elizabeth Barret. *Auroa Leigh.* VII, Line 820. Oxford University Press, 1993.

Why Me?

Kazantzakis, Nikos. *The Saviors of God; Spiritual Exercises,* translated by Kimon Friar. New York: Simon & Schuster, 1960.

Dossey, Larry. *Healing Words: The Power of Prayer and the Practice of Medicine.* San Francisco: HarperSanFrancisco, 1993.

Disappointment

Clark, Elizabeth, Ph.D. From handout at a Minn. conference for oncology caregivers, April, 1995.

Anger

Ith, Ian, and others. "Breast Cancer: The faces behind the Battle," *Seattle Times.* 13 September 1998, sec. L, pp. 1-3. Used by permission.

Make Today Count <http://userpages.itis.com/lemoll/index.html>

Despair

Hamilton, Robert Browning. "Along the Road," *The Best Loved Poems of the American People,* compiled by Hazel Felleman. Garden City, N.Y.: Doubleday, 1974.

Herhold, Robert. *Learning to Die; Learning to Live.* Philadelphia: Fortress Press, 1976.

Tatelbaum, Judy. *The Courage to Grieve.* New York: Lippincott & Crowell, 1980.

Grief

Sims, Darcie. "The Grief Process," *The Compassionate Friends Newsletter.* Winter 1988.

Humor

Cohn, Victor. "Releasing the Power of Hope," *Washington Post.* 2 June 1992.

Cousins, Norman. *Anatomy of an Illness as Perceived by the Patient: Reflections on Healing and Regeneration.* New York: Norton, 1979.

Lewis, Young Fio Rito. *Laugh, Clown, Laugh.* Warner Bros. Inc., 1928.

Pain

Welle, Janice, O.S.F. (n.p., n.d.).

Broyssenko, Joan, Ph.D. *Fire in the Soul: A New Psychology of Spiritual Optimism.* N.Y.: Warner Books, 1991.

Remen, Rachel Naomi. *Kitchen Table Wisdom: Stories That Heal.* New York: Riverhead Books, 1996.

Rabindranath, Tagore. "The Grasp of Your Hand," *The Heart of God: Prayers of Rabindranath Tagore.* Selected and edited by Herbert F. Vetter. Boston: Charles E. Tuttle Co. Inc., 1997.

Readiness

Beattie, Melody. *The Language of Letting Go.* Center City, Minn.: Hazelden, 1990.

Berg, Elizabeth. *Talk Before Sleep.* New York: Random House, 1994.

Noll, Peter. *In the Face of Death.* New York: Penguin Books, 1990.

Dying Rights

Kairos, 114 Douglass St., San Francisco, Calif. 94114

Dying Persons Bill of Rights. Created at a workshop on "The Terminally Ill Patient and the Helping Person," in Lansing, Mich. Sponsored by the Southwestern Michigan Inservice Council and conducted by Amelia J. Barbus, associate professor of nursing, Wayne State University, Detroit. As published in *Cancer Care*

Nursing by Marilee Ivers Donovan and Sandra Erdene Girton. New York: Appleton-Century-Crofts, 1984.

Soul Care
Emerson, Ralph Waldo. *Self-Reliance: The Wisdom of Ralph Waldo Emerson as Inspiration for Daily Living.* Selected by Richard Whelan. New York: Bell Tower, 1991.
Moore, Thomas. *Care of the Soul: A Guide for Cultivating Depth and Sacredness in Everyday Life.* New York: HarperCollins, 1992.
Williamsen, Joanne. *Lakeview Hospice Newsletter.* Stillwater, Minn., June 1998.

Dance
Kübler-Ross, Elisabeth. *The Wheel of Life.* N.Y.: Scribner, 1997.
Rodegast, Pat and Judith Stanton. *Emmanuels Book II: The Choice for Love.* N.Y.: Bantam Books, 1989.

Hospice
Saunders, Dame Cicely in *The Hospice Movement: A Better Way of Caring for the Dying* by Sandol Stoddard. New York: Vintage Books, 1992.

Spirit
The Bhagavad-Gita (500 B.C.). Sacred Hindu Text, translated by Winthrop Sargeant, State University of New York Press, chapter 2:20, 1984.

Memories
Jones, Rikki Lee, "Life's Little Reminders." Copyright © 1997 Compendium, Inc.

Legacy
Jewish Prayer, found in *I Remember You: A Grief Journal.* San Francisco: HarperSanFrancisco, 1995.

Unfinished Business
The Mom's Devotional Bible, New International Version. Grand Rapids, Mich.: The Zondervan Corp., 1996. Used by permission.
Dunn County Herald, Vol. 84, #50. 22 January 1999. Used by permission.
The Dream Foundation <http://www.firstcall.org/irisdb/p0000576.htm>
The Make-A-Wish Foundation <http://www.makeawish-la.org>

Gatherings
Maeterlinck, Maurice. *Our Eternity.* New York: Dodd, Mead & Company, 1914.
Trelease, Murray. "Dying Among Alaskan Indians: A Matter of Choice," *Death, The Final Stage of Growth* by Elisabeth Kübler-Ross. Englewood Cliffs, N.J.: Prentice Hall, 1975.

Hope
Cohn, Victor. "Releasing the Power of Hope." *Washington Post,* 2 June 1992.

Beyond This Life
Dickinson, Emily. #500. *Final Harvest, Emily Dickinson's Poems.* Compiled by Thomas H. Johnson. Boston: Little, Brown & Co., 1961.
Rodegast, Pat and Judith Stanton. *Emmanuel's Book: A Manuel for Living Comfortably in the Cosmos.* New York: Bantam Books, 1985.

Letting Go
Rinpoche, Sogyal. *The Tibetan Book of Living and Dying.* San Francisco: HarperSanFrancisco, 1993.
Beattie, Melody. *The Language of Letting Go.* Center City, Minn.: Hazelden, 1990.

Going Home
Rodegast, Pat and Judith Stanton. *Emmanuel's Book: A Manuel for Living Comfortably in the Cosmos.* New York: Bantam Books, 1985.
Menten, Ted. *Gentle Closings: How to Say Goodbye to Someone You Love.* Philadelphia, Pa.: Running Press, 1991.
Tagore, Rabindranath. *Light on Aging and Dying.* Compiled by Helen Nearing. Gardiner, Maine: Tilbury House, 1995.

Stories
O'Toole, Donna. See for example, *Aarvy Aardvark Finds Hope.* Burnsville, N.C.: Compassion Publishing, 1988.